Women in Work in Mid-Life

Drawing on a unique dataset of real women and their experiences of engaging in paid and unpaid work, *Women in Work in Mid-Life* explores the specific challenges that women in the UK workforce face, and reports on the value, identity and perception of mid-later life women at work.

From pay inequality and gender bias to the struggle to balance work and family life, the experience of women in the UK workforce is complex and multi-faceted. We live in an economic climate where the population and workforce is ageing, and the over-50s are encouraged by governments to engage more fully in paid work. However, the path to achieve this is unclear. Through interviews with women in work, as well as an examination of policies and initiatives that can help support women's career development and encourage workplace retention, it points to a future for this demographic in employment.

Women in Work in Mid-Life is an invaluable resource for professionals and policy-makers seeking to promote gender equality and create a more inclusive workplace culture in the UK, as well as undergraduate and graduate students of management, psychology and the social sciences.

Belinda Steffan is Research Fellow at the University of Edinburgh Business School. She researches how psychological and sociological experiences of gender, age and health at work influence continued labour force participation, or specifically, how women work. She is particularly interested in individual differences within the organisational context of work.

Women in Work in Mid-Life

Value, Identity and Perceptions

Belinda Steffan

Routledge
Taylor & Francis Group
LONDON AND NEW YORK

First published 2025
by Routledge
4 Park Square, Milton Park, Abingdon, Oxon OX14 4RN

and by Routledge
605 Third Avenue, New York, NY 10158

Routledge is an imprint of the Taylor & Francis Group, an informa business

British Library Cataloguing-in-Publication Data
A catalogue record for this book is available from the British Library

Library of Congress Cataloging-in-Publication Data
Names: Steffan, Belinda, author.
Title: Women in work in mid-life : value, identity and perceptions / Belinda Steffan.
Description: Abingdon, Oxon ; New York, NY : Routledge, 2025. | Includes bibliographical references and index.
Identifiers: LCCN 2024026976 (print) | LCCN 2024026977 (ebook) | ISBN 9781032574134 (hardback) | ISBN 9781032569635 (hardback) | ISBN 9781003439257 (ebook)
Subjects: LCSH: Middle-aged women—Employment—Great Britain. | Women employees—Great Britain. | Sex discrimination in employment—Great Britain. | Work and family—Great Britain.
Classification: LCC HD6056.2.G7 S739 2025 (print) | LCC HD6056.2.G7 (ebook) | DDC 331.4084/60941—dc23/eng/20240627
LC record available at https://lccn.loc.gov/2024026976
LC ebook record available at https://lccn.loc.gov/2024026977

ISBN: 9781032574134 (hbk)
ISBN: 9781032569635 (pbk)
ISBN: 9781003439257 (ebk)

DOI: 10.4324/9781003439257

Typeset in Sabon
by Apex CoVantage, LLC

Contents

Acknowledgement

I would like to thank my research mentor and supervisor over the years of developing my research on women in mid- to later life. Professor Wendy Loretto is a role model for women supporting other women, and for this, I am thankful.

1 Introduction

More women in mid- to later life are in paid employment than any time in history, and the number of women at work is only going to increase. Global population ageing has led to workforce population ageing in the majority of countries around the world. The ageing population is a global challenge, however, enabling women in mid- to later life to engage more fully with paid work, can also be seen as a political, economic, social and individual opportunity. I say 'enabling' as it is not enough to expect women to engage in paid work without addressing – or being blind to – structural constraints. And I say 'paid work' acknowledging that women still perform the majority of unpaid work such as caring, housework and emotional labour.

Research on labour market participation of 'older workers' has been active over the past two decades, with seminal work distilling findings down to one key point – mid-life workers are individuals and have unique challenges based on a range of life course and demographic factors, and yet they are more often than not collectively analysed and described as an homogenous, gender-neutral body of labour (Taylor et al., 2016). As such, focus on women and age groups within the mid- to later life stage is timely and important.

Books have been published that focus on women at work, although these are generally around how to climb the corporate leader and be 'successful' – whatever that means to people. My research suggests that women over 40 have an appetite for a book about work that does not focus on climbing and focuses on supporting them to stay at work through the challenging stage of mid-life when competing challenges of health, family, financial situation and the domestic context can threaten how women engage with paid work. This information is just as relevant for managers, academics and policy-makers who are interested in workplace retention of this growing and increasingly important demographic of the labour market.

Women in Work in Mid-Life positions women's ageing at work at the centre of an exploration of mid- to later life worker identity carried out through identity work and liminality, or the transitional nature of ageing at work. Specifically, this is an investigation into how women in mid- to later life internalise gendered ageism through bodily ageing at work. Internalised

DOI: 10.4324/9781003439257-1

ageism has been exposed as a 'social problem' experienced through the body (Hurd Clarke & Korotchenko, 2016; Hurd Clarke & Griffin, 2008) and conducted through a social construction of what it means to be 'older' (Phelan, 2018). Research has largely focused on how health, age and gender play a significant role in employment outcomes of workers in mid- to later life (Edge et al., 2017; Taylor et al., 2016; Loretto & Vickerstaff, 2015, 2013; Sanders & McCready, 2010). However, few work-related studies have explored the relationship workers in mid- to later life have with their ageing bodies at work (Bowman et al., 2016) or the mechanism of perceptions behind how and why women in mid- to later life internalise ageist assumptions.

1.1 Context: United Kingdom

This book focuses on the United Kingdom (UK) context, which is currently experiencing an ageing workforce but also has some significant labour market shortfalls due to a number of factors including changes in government policy and comparative workplace conditions such as pay. While this book is arguably UK-centric, the findings and key messages can apply to any global context with similar political, social and economic challenges around labour markets and the economic activity of their ageing population.

While workers over 50 comprise almost one-third of the workforce, claims of a 'Great Unretirement' to meet labour shortfalls in almost all sectors of the UK economy are premature: there are still more economically inactive workers over 50 now than pre-pandemic (Centre for Ageing Better, 2023). The UK Government have focused policy on the recruitment, retraining and retention of workers over 50 since they launched their extending working lives (EWL) initiative in 2015 (Altmann, 2015), renamed more recently by the Department of Work and Pensions to '50+ Choices', which was recently refreshed with the Spring Budget (UK Government, 2023). The Spring Budget highlighted that the UK's labour market needs more workers, and explicitly identified the need for 'older workers' – workers over 50 – to increase their economic activity. However, there seems to be some disconnect between the UK Government's current mantra of asking workers over 50 to come back to work, with catchy slogans such as 'Britain needs you' (Byrne, 2023) and the readiness of UK employers to recruit and retain workers in mid- to later life.

In *Women in Work in Mid-Life*, I argue that more policy focus should be on the latter, as we should not assume that all workers have the choice and control to simply return to work should they so desire. There is a clear business case to support workers in mid- to later life. One-third of UK businesses have recently reported that they are experiencing a shortage of workers (Office for National Statistics, 2023). To solve these issues, we must put emphasis on joined up thinking between government policy, employer policy and approach strategic and operational human resources management (HRM) practices focusing on the needs and wants of 'older workers', but not as an homogenous body of labour (Taylor et al., 2016). The reality is, in fact, far more complicated, and this book only has space within its 70,000-odd words to shine a light on one key area in need of more attention, i.e. to improve how women in mid- to later life are valued at work – by themselves and by others.

While EWL initiatives focus on financial security and overall health and well-being, knowledge of the impact of gendered ageing on women's working lives 'is fragmented and limited', and an overarching perspective on women's health and work ability is largely missing (see Gjellestad et al., 2023 for a recent scoping review). As health is a key determinant of being economically active in mid- to later life, it is also crucial to consider women's health when asking questions around how women work.

1.2 Why women, and why now?

Why women? Women in mid- to later life have been identified as having the potential to address identified labour market gaps. When I read about how women in mid- to later life work, I find myself reading the word 'gap' a lot. Women have a pay gap and pension gap; there are gendered data gaps, health gaps, government policy gaps. Why do women experience all of these gaps? And crucially, are we reporting on the 'right' gaps?

The gender seniority gap is still a cause for concern. We are still seeing evidence that women are not seen as 'suitable' or desired for senior management roles. One recent study found that 15% of HR managers still believe that men are better suited than women for senior manager roles. We know from previous research that findings such as this are largely industry-specific; however, gendered assumptions about women in senior roles is still as issue for many women at work (Fawcett Society, 2023). This seniority gap contributes to the gender pay gap.

The gender pay gap was recently reported as unlikely to achieve parity until 2051 (Fawcett Society, 2023). Their report found that women currently aged 40 and over will not experience an equity in gender pay differences in their working lives. It is unclear what path we need to take as a society to achieve this by 2051. Women in paid employment earn on average £29,684 a year, compared with £35,260 a year earned by men, according to the analysis of official data by the Trades Union Congress (TUC). Analysis of figures from the Office for National Statistics found the gender divide on pay was widest for women aged between 50 and 59, who suffer a pay gap of 20.8% – the equivalent of working 76 days a year for free – while women aged over 60 had a gender pay gap of 18.4% (The Guardian, February 2023).

The gender caring gap – whereby women still do the majority of unpaid caring through an often implied gendered household contract – is one of the most commonly discussed reasons behind gender pay gaps. While there are mechanisms of the unspoken societal rules of the gendered household contract behind how this manifests in households throughout the land, it is of concern because unpaid caring is still insufficiently considered by economists as part of the gross domestic product (GDP) question, and those hours spent on unpaid care do not count (i.e. are not valued) as economically active. A recent report (Carers UK, 2022) found that 40% of the 10,751 unpaid carers in their survey, who are employees with unpaid caring roles, are (considering) leaving paid work, and a further 22% are considering reducing their hours. This report reminds us of the knock-on effect of caring for others on other aspects of life – health, well-being, financial precarity. There is a clear impact of unpaid caring on health (almost one-third of carers report bad or very bad mental health) and on financial well-being/precarity (75% of unpaid carers are struggling to pay their own bills).

This gender inequality is underpinned by some fundamental gender data gaps. There remains a lack of data on how women in mid- to later life work. Specifically, there are data gaps on women's general health (Criado-Perez, 2019). It was recently reported (Hill, 2023) that Professor Geeta Nargund, the author of the foreword to the 'Women Count' report, stated that 'One of the conclusions that is inescapable from the data is that women count, but men count more'. This is disturbing to read on a number of levels, so I investigated how researchers capture data on women's health in mid- to later life in the UK, focusing on menopause as my main area of academic interest. This is what I found:

Understanding Society (2023), Wave 13. I made a word search for 'health' and there were 226 items, 82 items for 'health condition', 24 items for 'mental health' and zero items for both of the terms 'women's health' and 'menopause'.

UK Biobank (2024) has one question on menopause, which is 'Had menopause?'

English Longitudinal Study of Ageing (ELSA, 2024) features menopause as a response to the question 'Were your periods stopped by . . . ?', but actually the response is written as 'the menopause (or no obvious reason)'. So, how could an analyst tease these apart? It is impossible to know if menopause or no obvious reason was the reason that a women's periods stopped.

We need to start collecting data on women's issues, women's health and women's choices so that we can better understand how mid-life women engage with work. It is difficult to attribute value to something if we do not measure it.

1.3 Complexity of mid- to later life for working women: 'messy lives'

At time of editing the final version of this book, I have interviewed hundreds and surveyed thousands of women in mid- to later life about their working lives. Very rarely do these women speak about work in isolation. Women's lives are complex, with each woman experiencing her own unique cocktail of work experiences, domestic context, health and well-being profile, unpaid caring responsibilities, individual differences (e.g. personality) and the life course story of how she made it through life to this point (e.g. early life, education, income, relationships, marital status, child-bearing etc.). The life stages of mid- to later life have a high hormonal impact through changing menstruation and menopause, which can influence our identity and sense of self (see Steffan, 2021 for a report on menopause). This is also a time when women's health around reproduction and (in)fertility might be especially salient and other aspects of health that are more common to the female than male body might be experienced more keenly (e.g. chronic pain, fatigue, endometriosis, fibromyalgia). As stated, women are still more likely to do the majority of unpaid care and domestic work, which can bring its own mental and physical health issues. We know that the majority of unpaid care is conducted by women, and while studies have focused on motherhood (Jones et al., 2023) and grandparent care (García-Jiménez et al., 2024), less is known about the gendered health implications of unpaid eldercare and other family care (siblings, adult children with or without special needs).

Financial precarity is an issue in mid- to later life, and the pension gap is higher for women over 50 in the UK than any other demographic. Financial well-being is more important to understand than ever before, given the current cost of living crisis in the UK and the majority of economies throughout the world. The causal relationship between worry around individual and household financial health and decreased self-reported health is well-established, and yet we know little about how this worry interacts with gendered health as women work in mid- to later life. Gendered ageism (i.e. the intersectional experiences of gender and age being more than the sum of its parts) is a thread that can unpin all of this complexity of life, making the

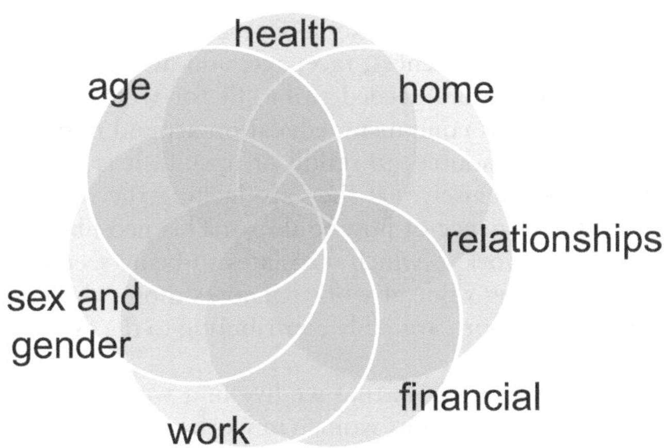

Figure 1.1 Women working in mid- to later life experience a complex web of interweaving psycho-social factors

smallest issues seem considerable. All of these factors can individually and intersectionally influence workplace experiences and retention (individual, organisational, economic). What remains unclear is how coping with this messiness of life interacts with work.

1.4 Whose responsibility is it to value women?

The majority of academic thinking and practical outputs follow a neo-liberal agenda, which is to put the onus of being 'fit for work' on the individual themselves. This provides the crux of the asymmetrical value proposition of women presented in this book. This message can come from a range of stakeholders, most significantly from current debates within government policy and organisational supports for health and well-being. Governments in their policies around the requirement of working longer with stretching out the state pension age (SPA) to 66 (currently) for women. Many organisations provide a wealth a well-meaning health and well-being supports via self-help portals or employee assistance programmes (EAPs), but require the individual to first understand their own health needs and second feel safe enough to ask for help. This can also come from the individual themselves. I have interviewed hundreds of women over the past few years, and the vast majority of women in these broad ranges of job types, socio-economic backgrounds and educational attainment have agentically placed the onus of being 'fit for work' and presenting their value to work on themselves as an individual. This neo-liberal, personal approach is arguably positioned within structural conditions, which I discuss in more detail in this book.

Personal responsibility alone is not sustainable, because investing in oneself can be costly in terms of time, money and effort. It also is not sustainable because focusing on personal responsibility for being 'fit for work' ignores structural barriers experienced by some women from marginalised groups: health, socio-economic differences, race, age, and disability. Not all women have access to the resources needed to be 'fit for work'. Resources might include money for fitness equipment, education around nutrition and availability of educational resources to reskill or upskill. It is not enough to expect women to help themselves if they are lacking the role models or the visible and tangible evidence of how to do so. This neo-liberal approach of women being 'fit for work' – which translates to being seen or perceived as possessing or embodying value at work – ignores those who need or at least would benefit from support, arguably contributing to the asymmetrical value proposition.

While we would like to think that we live in a world in which organisations and their structures support women in work out of goodwill or because it is the right thing to do, I am often asked for the business case around supporting women at work. I am clearly not alone in this experience as there has been a recent surge of evidence to encourage businesses to support the health and well-being of their workforce. In the section that follows, I will provide some key insights from recent reporting around why it is important for organisations to invest in their workforce.

It is interesting to note that the business case clearly suggests that retaining workers is cheaper than replacing workers through expensive recruitment policies. In April 2023, Business in the Community published a report with research from McKinsey Health Institute which provided some key insights into the value of retaining workers, reporting the cost of replacing a worker instead of retention (Business in the Community, 2023). It is also interesting to note that the focus of these initiatives can speak to any age group and are not specific to women – and this is a key point. The workplace policies that are required for women in mid-later life to feel that they can speak up about concerns around gendered ageism, menopause, responsibilities of unpaid care and stresses arising from relationship disruption can be translated to a broad range of workers. This reinforces the message that supporting women in mid- to later life at work is less about products and services and more about creating a supportive and inclusive organisational (or team) culture.

1.5 Aims of this book

Women in Work in Mid-Life provides insight on how women in mid- to later work, targeted at a range of audiences. As such, I have provided a full account of study design and method for researchers, students and practitioners who wish to conduct their own studies into how women work. Further, I have provided findings from a qualitative and a mixed-methods study to showcase different approaches to data collection and reporting. I summarise with a research agenda at the end of this book, with a hope that this book will encourage others to collect data and report on women over 40 who are the fastest growing sector of the labour market, and who are simultaneously inadequately understood while being called upon to rescue to the UK economy.

It is this point that drives the central message of this book. Women in mid-to later life have value – value to organisations, to society and to government. I argue that this value is largely untapped potential as structural barriers such as gendered ageism are holding this value from being recognised, even by the individual woman herself. *Women in Work in Mid-Life* aims to raise awareness of factors that influence how women in mid- to later life work, with the modest goal of guiding those who manage women at work and the lofty ambition of positively contributing to the economic outlook of the UK.

The book is presented as two studies.

Study 1 provides detail of an investigation into mid-life experiences of ageing at work, looking at less-discussed issues specific to women in mid- to later life. This is because much of the current understanding of women in mid- to later life is through studies of 'older workers', which insufficiently considers gender differences and inadequately considers differences in age over 50.

Study 2 sought to explore the concept of value more explicitly. Specifically, Study 2 was designed to explore the role of gender in how value was perceived by women themselves. Study 2 sought to better understand how women understand or even create perceived value at work through perceptions of mainly out-group others, how they perceive being economically active and how neo-liberal attitudes of personal work ethic and personal responsibilities surrounding an asymmetrical value proposition are expressed. To that end, Study 2 sought to understand *the relational experience* of women in mid- to later life, beyond the heterogeneity of the majority of approaches to manage and make policy around women in mid- to later life.

When I was thinking about the title for this book, I was tempted to call it 'It's not all about gender, but it actually kind of is', which, while not particularly academic, is an accurate summary of the findings in both Study 1 and Study 2. The point is that Study 1 found that perceptions and meta-perceptions (what we think others are thinking of us) are largely in relation to younger others at work, much of the narrative of the participants was rooted in (internalised) gendered ageism. Similarly, Study 2's key finding was that women were more interested in the fairness of pay relative to a range of factors, and the gender pay gap was not high on that list. And yet, again, much of the sentiment around working in mid- to later life was through the life course accumulated (dis)advantage of being a woman and being older, relatively speaking.

Women in Work in Mid-Life reaches out to a range of audiences. These include the following (in no particular order):

- Government policy-makers – we need policy that goes beyond 'older workers' as heterogenous labour (Taylor et al., 2016) and considers the working lives of women differently from that of men. Policy should also consider the over-40s, as this mid-life phase is lacking as much focus as 'younger' and 'older' workers.
- Senior managers of organisations who are wanting (or needing) to retain or recruit women in mid- to later life due to overall staff shortfalls. In the current economic climate, I would suggest this is a high proportion of organisations.
- Strategic HRM and senior executives in charge of people.
- HRMs, focusing on the legal and operational aspects of people management.
- Academics – we need inter-disciplinary research on how women in mid- to later life work. I would encourage psychologists, sociologists and management theorists to engage with a range of other disciplines to be more creative in how we do our research.
- Line managers – there is increasing pressure on line managers to be a 'one-stop shop' for supporting employees. While an individual's experience at work is highly associated with whether or not they have a 'good' line manager, we must also ensure that line managers are supported with knowledge and time in order to be a 'good' line manager on top of their own work.

- Women in mid- to later life themselves – women need to better understand their value in the world of paid work.

1.6 Policy focus: extending working lives

This research is important because extending working lives of workers in mid- to later life is a current and major economic, social and individual focus, requiring a more thorough and nuanced understanding of factors affecting attitudes towards work. The main aim of this book is to explore how women's experiences of bodily ageing and internalised ageism influences attitudes towards their participation in the paid labour force and extending their working lives. While this book is UK-centric, the findings within can translate to many other countries around the world, as an ageing population and subsequent ageing workforce has been identified as a global challenge, but has also been identified as an opportunity (UK Parliament, 2023; OECD, 2023). I quite often say that menopausal women can save the UK economy, and this book goes some way to showing how.

Due to an ageing population, workers in mid- to later life are the fastest-growing sector of labour force participation. There are now over 24 million people aged over 50 years in the United Kingdom (UK), more than one-third of the UK population (Age UK, 2018). For the first time in history, there are more than 10 million people aged over 50 in employment, making up 31% of the entire UK workforce, an increase from 21% in the early 1990s (Office for National Statistics, 2016). Further, it is estimated that by 2040, 40% of total earned income in the UK will be generated by workers over 50, which is an increase from 23% in 2004 and 30% in 2018 (International Longevity Centre, 2019). As such, delaying retirement and extending working lives of the older worker is the subject of intense social and economic focus, which indeed has been a topic of increasing focus for the past decade (Loretto & Vickerstaff, 2013, 2015).

Workers have different motivations for extending their working lives (Freund, 2006; Kooij et al., 2011). Many workers find themselves working longer due to financial necessity. For example, Truxillo et al. (2015) reported that 60% of workers aged 45–74 were working primarily for financial need. Winkelmann-Gleed (2012), however, found that balancing work commitments with other aspects of identity (family, social) resulted in higher workplace commitment, and called for studies into labour force participation to move away from financial motives behind how people in mid- to later life work. Work is also important to individuals as they age as a source of social status, self-esteem and a route to productive ageing (Sabelis & Schilling, 2013) and perceived life course advantages, such as the ability to choose work based on enjoyment or other personal motivation (Unson & Richardson, 2012; Kooij et al., 2011; Freund, 2006).

The employment trajectory for women – more than men – continues to be uneven and stalled, resulting in significant gendered inequality in labour force participation across adulthood, showing a cumulative and lasting effect of work gaps largely due to gendered domestic constraints (Loretto & Vickerstaff, 2013; Damaske, 2011; Damaske & Frech, 2016). The gendered bifurcation of the labour market is increasingly divided into part-time, temporary work, which is generally low paid (Gray & Kish-Gephart, 2013; Riach et al., 2015), and different career composition due to 'patchwork' or interrupted and non-linear careers (Sabelis & Schilling, 2013). Further, Schilling (2015) posited that highly qualified women violate social norms around biographical work-life balance, where career trajectories – often mapped against those of men – are interrupted due to child-bearing and child-rearing: female workers have to work longer and harder to operate at the same level as men.

At the time of writing this book, there is a vibrant social media campaign reporting that 22 November is the day when women start to 'work for free' compared with men due to the gender pay gap (Fawcett Society, 2023). The gender pay gap is improving in many sectors, but there remains a difference in how much women are paid for the same work compared with men. Gender equality is a barrier to working longer and is made up of a myriad of gendered factors. The gender employment gap accounts for 14.5% fewer female workers aged 55–64 years (Edge et al., 2017). The gender pay gap in the UK was 7.7% in April 2023 for all ages, but was reported as 10.3% for 40–49 year olds and 14.2% for over 60s, so while an improvement from 21% in 2008 (Office for National Statistics, 2023, 2016), there is still clearly room for improvement.

Structural barriers impacting women in mid- to later life include the extension of the SPA designed to encourage individuals to extend their working lives. The SPA for women has recently disproportionately increased from 60 to 66 and will likely increase further to 68 in the next few decades (Age UK, 2020). While this can be viewed as a correction to align with men, bringing gender equality to the SPA, it is arguably a more dramatic increase for the current cohort of women, whose expected pensionable age has increased by almost one decade. Designed to stem increasing pension costs and realise potential labour market supply, female workers have already responded to the call to 'work harder for longer', whereby female labour force participation increased by 29% between 1985 and 2009 and hours of work increased by 62% (Bell & Hart, 2010); labour supplied by women over 50 more than doubled in that period. Despite the quantity of research into working in later life, there exists a clear requirement for researchers and practitioners to move away from the model of viewing workers in mid- to later life as a homogenous, gender-neutral body of labour (Taylor et al., 2016).

Individual and gendered structural factors around extending working lives and labour force participation of workers in mid- to later life highlight the need for a more nuanced understanding how women work (Damaske & Frech, 2016; Riach et al., 2015; Loretto & Vickerstaff, 2013; Gray & Kish-Gephart, 2013; Sabelis & Schilling, 2013). As such, this book focuses on the individual as its primary unit of enquiry. Further, responding to the call for work-related research to consider broader structural effects (Alvesson et al., 2008), this book also considers the worker and their individual factors within their organisational context. Specifically, this book explores the interaction between the ageing body at work and the transitional nature of bodily ageing at work through liminality and identity work, with a view of exploring internalised gendered ageism and mechanisms which drive identity work, including the role of perceptions of self (self-identity) and others (social identity) (Beech, 2011)

1.7 Two studies presented in this book

1.7.1 *Study 1: an exploratory qualitative investigation into mid-life women's experiences of ageing at work*

A central aim of this book is to explore how concepts of identity affected mid-life women's attitudes towards continued labour force participation, and how such influencing factors affecting work identity are understood, internalised and performed. The gendered, ageing body is at the heart of this enquiry due to its centrality into how women perceive themselves and are perceived at work in terms of differential perceptions of performance and fit with organisational culture and expectations (Steffan, 2021; Calasanti & King, 2018; Hurd Clarke, 2018; Isopahkala-Bouret, 2017; Carter, 2016; Zacher, 2015; Sabelis & Schilling, 2013; Tulle & Krekula, 2013; Trethewey, 1999). This book responds to the imperative to look beyond the gender-neutral older body (Taylor et al., 2016; Emslie & Hunt, 2009; Loretto & Vickerstaff, 2013) to study gender and age together as part of a whole to explore how different forms of inequality affect each other (Riach et al., 2015).

Women in Work in Mid-Life is a study of women, positioned as such due to the life course experiences of being women and how this culminates in gendered experiences in mid- to later life. This is not to undermine experiences of non–cis-gender women, it is simply that the life course experiences of women who might have experienced gender-based discrimination, constrained choice, implicit control and workplace penalties are relevant to this specific study.

What is less explored and often neglected is the role of the gendered ageing body in the reality of gender inequality of women who work in mid- to later life (Bowman et al., 2016). While there are some positive individual tales of ageing at work (Krekula, 2016), and certainly this is becoming the case more recently (Butler, 2020; Quental et al., 2023), the overwhelming narrative within many places and spaces of work is the ageing body in performative decline (Riach, 2007, Thomas et al., 2014). Women tend to be judged more harshly for their ageing bodies than men (Sontag, 1979; Krekula, 2016; Cameron et al., 2019), but what is not clear is what impact this difference has on individual experiences of female workers in terms of employment retention and extension of working lives. Studies of work have shied away from highlighting the role of the gendered ageing body (Bowman et al., 2016), despite evidence highlighting the centrality of the body to work, encouraging this age-based research into how women in mid- to later life work.

It became clear from my literature review of previous academic studies, and from my initial analyses of the data, that perceptions played a specific and significant role in individual worker experience of ageing and in workplace engagement. Specifically, early data analyses revealed that perceptions around bodily ageing were important to participants in how they engaged with their highly contextualised world of work. This iterative process of initial data analysis and ongoing background research through developing the literature review contributed to the following overarching research objective of Study 1.

Research objective (a): How do women in mid- to later life experience the transitional nature of ageing in relation to their bodily ageing at work?

Research objective (b): How do these gendered experiences operate to internalise gendered ageism through the active exploration of work identity (identity work)?

Workers over 50 have been and continue to be actively encouraged to extend their working lives up to and even beyond the revised SPA, but not without critique as to its practicality (Bell & Hart, 2010; Byrne, 2023). As such, it is timely to ask questions about perceptions of how the gendered ageing body is able to accommodate this additional temporal component within the same job, organisation and industry. This inevitably raises questions around how workers in mid- to later life view their current and future labour force participation, specifically around workplace retention (Altmann, 2015). As UK Government resources are now focused on workers over 50, as the Department of Work and Pensions 'leads [the] way supporting people aged over 50 at work' (UK Government, February 2023), we ask some specific questions about how they should go about doing this to maximise benefit to the individual worker.

The role of not only perceptions of self but the importance that participants placed on the perceptions of others in relation to their physical appearance at work: perceptions of others appeared to drive decisions around labour force participation. This question was not part of the original study and only emerged after initial data coding. Perceptions around appearance are clearly important, as appearance bias is controlled by taste-based judgements made with little other relevant information (Hosoda et al., 2003). The literature on perceptions of others, meta-perceptions (Carlson et al., 2011; Meister et al., 2017) or reflected appraisal (McMullin & Cairney, 2004) suggests that individuals internalise perceptions of others, which might affect self-esteem, productivity, performance, ability and continuity at work

(Grandey et al., 2020; Hickey et al., 2017; Bariola et al., 2017; Howlett et al., 2015), work identity transition (Ibarra, 1999) and idealised identity or striving for 'optimal distinctiveness' (Beech, 2008; Brewer, 1991). What is unclear from these studies is how these aspects of perception of self and others affect not only worker identity but practical employment outcomes. To that end, the following research question emerged as relevant and important to this enquiry.

Emerging research question: 'How, why and from whom do women in mid- to later life draw on perceptions of self and others through bodily ageing to engage in their world of work?'

1.7.2 *Study 2: a mixed-methods investigation into understanding value as fairness of mid-life women at work*

Study 2 comprised of a survey looking at how women over 40 work, which included questions around health and well-being at work, psychological capital, burnout, workplace engagement and performance, and how much unpaid care is performed while engaging in paid work. I also asked a range of open text questions around work 'gaps'. Specifically, these questions were designed to elicit a response to any factors that contribute positively and negatively to engaging in paid work now and in the future.

The criteria for survey inclusion were simply for the participant to identify as a woman, be in paid employment and be over 40 years of age. The survey was completed by 511 women working in the UK in a range of industries and job types, who all provided survey responses (quantitative data) and also open text responses (qualitative data). This book provides evidence on one aspect of the survey from Study 2, linking to the concept of value from Study 1, which relates specifically to attitudes to fair pay (i.e. value).

Together, Study 1 and Study 2 address an explicit need for both individual workers and organisations to better understand factors affecting women in mid- to later life towards their continued and future labour force participation, specifically demonstrating how to value women in mid- to later life at work.

1.8 A note on the COVID-19 pandemic

This is not a book about how the COVID-19 pandemic changed work – that subject is covered in an increasing number of books, journal articles and blogs elsewhere. Indeed, I co-authored a chapter on lessons learned from COVID-19 for women working through menopause, which I encourage anyone working in the education sector to read (Steffan & Potočnik, 2023). However, it would be remiss of me not to address the role that the COVID-19 pandemic played on the data collection and analysis in both Study 1 and Study 2 of this book, and also to experiences of how women in mid- to later life work.

There are a number of ways that the COVID-19 pandemic influences women in mid- to later life that are outside the scope of this book. For example, the pandemic has put significant pressure on the National Health Service (NHS). Evidence suggests that women wait longer than men to be admitted to emergency medical care in Scotland. Since COVID-19, women's average waiting time can be up to 44 minutes longer than men's waiting time for some health departments and can exacerbate already existing health inequalities (The Ferret, 2023). In terms of the gender pay gap, at the start of the pandemic (March 2020), more women than men were furloughed, suggesting a deepening of the gender pay gap (Business in the Community, 2023). It is interesting to note that this article refers to progress being made in addressing fair pay, which it does through rooting fairness in gender pay disparity.

Study 1 data collection was finished prior to 2020, so experiences and narratives in Study 1 do not reflect COVID-19 in any way. The analysis, writing up and presentation of these data were done during COVID-19, which could have put a slight twist on how information was received by audiences of presentations; however, that has not influenced findings presented in this book. The design of Study 2 was conducted during late 2022 and early 2023, and as such incorporated overall experiences of a change of how work could be done – specifically, access to flexible work. The study design and development of research questions themselves do not explicitly relate to COVID-19; however, we cannot ignore that many women in mid- to later life will have changed how they work since the pandemic.

2 Literature review

2.1 Gendered ageing at work

The ageing body is firmly at the centre of this enquiry into how workers in mid- to later life experience perceptions around ageing, addressing a lacuna in the field of organisational studies and highlighting a call by researchers to reject the view of workers in mid- to later life as a homogenous, gender-neutral body of labour (Taylor et al., 2016). The body – more specifically, the relationship workers have with their ageing bodies – has been largely absent from organisational literature. This is surprising, given that the body is so fundamental to a worker's sense of identity (Calasanti & King, 2018; Carter, 2016), association of aesthetic labour with commercial gain (Warhurst et al., 2009), perceived and internalised age discrimination (Hurd Clarke, 2018) and performativity of age(ing) in society and work through the body (Calasanti & King, 2018; Isopahkala-Bouret, 2017; Tulle & Krekula, 2013; Trethewey, 1999).

Ageing is a time of change, through which work identities might be challenged. As such, this book draws on liminal identity work theory (Beech, 2011) to understand how women experience, manage and present their ageing bodies at work through the 'ongoing mental activity that an individual undertakes in constructing an understanding of self that is coherent, distinct and positively valued' (Alvesson et al., 2008). This definition captures several key aspects relating to bodily ageing at work: agency, (re)construction of self-identity and social identity, and the perceived value of the worker.

Individuals reflexively attach meaning to themselves through identity construction (Brown, 2015), subjective interpretations of who they are relevant to their environments (Caza et al., 2018), but what is less clear is the source of these meanings, from whom perceptions are sought and what impact do these perceptions have on worker identity, continued labour force participation and factors leading to early exit from the workplace. It is the agentic process of these active and fluid interpretations and external discourses which are available to and imposed upon individuals (Ybema et al., 2009; Beech, 2011) that encourages this investigation into how women in mid- to later life engage in 'identity work', which is the term used for the gamut of

DOI: 10.4324/9781003439257-2

agentic behaviours in which an individual engages to construct, shape, maintain, reinforce or work on personal identities with regard to their image of self and perceptions of others (Coupland & Brown, 2012).

Due to the transitional nature of ageing, or becoming older at work (Hurd Clarke, 2018) where work identities are 'ad hoc and positional' (Brown, 2015, p. 23) and are arguably an emotional experience (Winkler, 2018; Caza et al., 2018), liminal identity work (Beech, 2011) is used to navigate through liminal transition periods (Ibarra & Obodaru, 2016) whereby workers in mid- to later life might find themselves 'neither one thing or the other' (Turner, 1969): older-not-old. To date, there is a limited body of work on liminal identity work practices conducted by workers over 50 in relation to perceptions of their ageing bodies (Foweraker & Cutcher, 2019).

In addition to the core theoretical concepts stated here, other factors which potentially affect work engagement through bodily ageing include perceptions of self and others around notions of successful ageing[1] and emotional responses to ageing. Successful ageing places the onus of responsibility of the individual through a neo-liberal narrative of harnessing personal and social resources, striving to be an 'ideal worker' (Zacher, 2015; Rowe & Kahn, 2015, 1997) through the association of positive health and youthful appearance (Cameron et al., 2019; Carter, 2016), largely ignoring emotional responses to the ageing body despite its role in value-seeking at work (Warhurst et al., 2009). Drawing on core literature around the ageing body at work, work identity and liminality, this book seeks to further explore these supporting factors affecting how women in mid- to later life work.

Ageing bodies are insufficiently openly discussed at work and in work-related research (Bowman et al., 2016); much of the research into older bodies has been conducted within the disciplines of sociology and social gerontology (Hurd Clarke, 2018; Krekula, 2016). Specifically, the role of women's bodies in how labour force participation decisions in mid- to later life are made is yet to be adequately explored within the context of work. Research to date has focused on productivity and objective bodily function, highlighting the perception of an ageing body as tantamount to 'degeneration and slowing down' (Riach, 2007), whereby aesthetic labour shapes employee relationships with their body (Warhurst et al., 2009). Ageing, as a transitional process, is often perceived as that which must be 'avoided, controlled, even cured' or in need of control, creating tensions around bodily ageing potentially resulting in lowered self-esteem (Carter, 2016).

Alongside this enduring narrative of decline, women in mid- to later life are expected to take defensive action to meet social and organisational expectations of age, perceived through the associations of positive health and youthful appearance (Thomas et al., 2014; Slevin, 2010; Hurd Clarke & Griffin, 2008). This uncertainty around performance of work identity through bodily changes in mid- to later life is a central component of the 'enduring constellation of attributes, beliefs, values, motives and experiences in terms of how people define themselves at work' (Ibarra, 1999, p. 764).

And yet, very little is written about how women in mid- to later life work (re)construct work identity in relation to an ageing body.

2.1.1 *The double standard of gendered ageing at work*

Early research into the ageing body presented a double standard of ageing whereby women are perceived as less attractive and productive as they age, while men – especially those with financial and social resources – can be held in esteem in later life despite signs of physiological ageing (Schein, 2007, 2001; Schein & Mueller, 1992; Sontag, 1979). For women, the body is regarded as a 'problematic object' (Krekula, 2016, p. 63), whereby women in mid- to later life experience greater body dissatisfaction with ageing (Cameron et al., 2019).

While women differentially experience employment outcomes due to physical ageing, Bowman et al. (2016) found that this difference was contingent upon industry context and occupational status. The authors found that only a minority of their 80 participants felt ageism in relation to being perceived as less fit, and this was a narrative conducted mainly by men in manual jobs; whereas women in mid- to later life in customer service roles felt 'invisible' due to a perceived desire from organisations and customers for a youthful aesthetic, which they felt that they no longer embodied. This gender distinction between 'rusty' men and 'invisible' women demonstrated how gendered ageing bodies were interpreted differently in terms of employability within organisational contexts; however, the authors presented relatively established gendered sex-type jobs, i.e. manual labour and shop sales. What remains unclear is how experiences of bodily ageing in a more diverse and gender-neutral range of work settings might present more subtle appearance-based challenges to women in mid- to later life.

It is, however, an oversimplification to discuss ageing simply as a negative outcome. Research from social gerontologists associates ageing with positive connotations such as being taken more seriously whereby positive presentations of the ageing body might lead to greater acceptance of ageing at work (Krekula, 2009; Isopahkala-Bouret, 2017). Krekula (2009) suggested that ageing is actually embraced by women in mid- to later life as a time of freedom, describing it as the 'best time of their lives'. For women, older is a time of paradox where people can 'no longer take youthful bodies for granted; changes in function and appearance mark them as no longer young' (Calasanti & King, 2018), and yet it is also a time of relative privilege for many.

Increasingly, we are seeing more academic literature being published on the positives of menopause, as a visible manifestation of women's bodily ageing, in the workplace. One notable article was published using Margaret Mead's concept of menopause zest (Quental et al., 2023). The authors challenge the pervasive bio-focused narrative of decline by demonstrating that experiences of menopause can be empowering, and encourage organisations to embrace the positive side of menopause, taking a more holistic view of the transition in the wider experiences of health in mid- to later life. Similarly,

Clare Butler (2020) has written about menopause as a gendered challenge relating to age, but that menopausal bodies and their association with gendered ageism can be harnessed as a form of (self) management and body activism, which offered women agency that might have otherwise or previously been compromised.

Bodies are gendered objects, leading to an expectation of bodily appearance based on group membership (Calasanti & King, 2018), such as age, gender or indeed the intersection of age and gender. The construction of the body is then an extension of self in how it is presented within the workplace (Warhurst et al., 2009). Tulle and Krekula (2013) remind us that the relationship we have with our bodies changes over time within the construct of social meanings: 'we do not invent them – we often reproduce them or others reproduce them through us'. Perceptions of the body are considered part of the myriad of factors that intertwine resulting in a potentially conflicting self-expression and conformity within the world of work.

2.2 Identity theory

The life course presents many twists and turns that women must navigate and negotiate within their work context. Women might need to overcome barriers to staying at work and extending their working lives should they wish to do so. Presentation of the ageing body is an intrinsic part of self and worker identity (Calasanti & King, 2018; Carter, 2016); as such, identity forms the central theoretical framework of this book. This literature review will next present the theoretical positioning of this book with identity, specifically identity work and liminality to highlight its relevance to bodily ageing at work.

In addressing the deceptively simple question of 'Who am I?', identity is a complex concept of self made up of social, personal, and role identities (Brown, 2015) and 'entwines feelings, values and behaviour . . . in sometimes conflicting directions' (Alvesson et al., 2008). It is generally accepted among identity scholars that self-identity is multi-dimensional and contextual, consisting of many different fluid and dynamic sub-identities (Miscenko & Day, 2016; Caza et al., 2018; Ashforth & Schinoff, 2016; Brown, 2015; Ashforth & Saks, 1995). Demographic characteristics, including age and gender, are a source of self-identity through attribution of personal meaning (Caza et al., 2018) and reflections of others (McMullin & Cairney, 2004). Ageing, due to its 'naturalised temporal component' leads people to avoid categorisation, as opposed to gender, where group members tend to identify themselves without hesitation (Calasanti & King, 2018). Broadly, identity offers a frame of 'great theoretical promise', providing a platform to build 'interesting empirical analyses' (Alvesson et al., 2008) and one that I use throughout this book to explore how women in mid- to later life work.

One key motivation of identity theory is self-verification, which is reliant on an aspect of change of self in alignment with perceived expectations of others (see Caza et al., 2018 for summary of key papers). I argue, therefore, that perceptions – specifically, perceptions of others – form the basis of identity as individuals' understanding of the perception of others offer motivation for agentic identity work within the structural confines of organisations and broader society. One approach to identity theory, narrative theory, focuses on individually and socially constructed stories used to make sense and communicate aspects of identity, which generally focuses on a personal narrative of self, or personal identity (Ibarra & Barbulescu, 2010). Narrative theory approaches can highlight the story an individual has constructed about themselves through relationality with others (Beech, 2008; Brown, 2001). This relationality, or positional power, can contribute to a discrepancy in how we see ourselves and how we believe we are seen by others (Meister et al., 2014). Further, it is interesting to note that the key motivation for narrative theory is coherence and plausibility (Alvesson & Wilmott, 2002; Brown, 2015; Caza et al., 2018): coherence is a consistency of self-identity narrative, but also a coherence between the self and one's environment. Further, plausibility over-rides the need for accuracy of a self-identity narrative (Caza et al., 2018), contributing to the question of how perceptions of self and others (Carlson et al., 2011) can influence our sense of self.

Narrative theory is a useful lens to understand the cumulative effects of an individual's life time of experiences – past, present and future as life course narratives are particularly relevant to individuals in mid- to later life (Tulle & Krekula, 2013). However, as individuals are motivated to 'see themselves as remaining the same over time' (Caza et al., 2018) through a comparison of oneself 'back in time' (Krekula, 2016), it could be suggested that identity work is used to find this coherence of self within a work context. Crucially, external discourses impressed upon individuals, which can then be internalised, can inform this personal identity narrative (Beech, 2011). Further, identity work is conducted through the discourses that are available to individuals (Ybema et al., 2009) at specific life course phases.

2.2.1 *Work identity and identity work*

Identity can be linked 'to nearly everything' in organisations (Caza et al., 2018; Alvesson et al., 2008). Identities are 'temporary, context-sensitive, an evolving set of constructions' and are 'ongoing internal soliloquies'; identity work is a continuous process (Alvesson et al., 2008, p. 15) ranging in activities including 'forming, repairing, maintaining, strengthening or revising' (Alvesson & Wilmott, 2002, p. 626). Work identities are complex self-meanings linked to labour force participation, compounding the social construct of self-identity with organisational culture and role identity of one's job. Further, a strong work identity can result in high job satisfaction and become a source of self-worth (Miscenko & Day, 2016), and yet, work identity is 'always provisional and contested' where the notion of enduring and stable work identity is denied by contemporary identity theorists (Brown, 2015).

Identity work is inherently performance based (Beech, 2008), conducted through discourse and personal narrative (Snow & Anderson, 1987; Alvesson et al., 2008) and through the physical self, or the body (Riach & Loretto, 2009). Identity work requires some control, for example, workers in mid- to later life who can agentically portray themselves as being active to demonstrate their value at work (Riach & Loretto, 2009). While control is often sought, identity work can involve 'chaotic, sometimes contradictory collections of self' (Alvesson et al., 2008; Jones & Clifton, 2018). For example, Ibarra (2015) posited that the managers in her study were aware that they must 'sell themselves' in order for their work to be recognised, also noting that workers struggled to self-promote until they established their value through experience.

Workers are expected to be agentic in forming and presenting who they are at work (Caza et al., 2018). Workers in mid- to later life are expected to take 'preventative' action to meet social and organisational constructs of 'older', perceived through the desirability of the appearance of youth from the older body (Hurd Clarke & Griffin, 2008; Slevin, 2010; Thomas et al., 2014). As work identity is grounded in the dominant social discourse as the legitimate discourse (Ybema et al., 2009; Cameron et al., 2019), it could be argued that the social construction of 'older' is internalised within an older worker's identity. An interesting example of this was presented by Ibarra (2015), who reported that her participant, a senior manager who found value in identifying as a maternal figure for her team, or as a 'mother hen with her chicks all around' – but this identity stopped being helpful when she hoped to transition from a team player to a more senior position. Her gendered identity narrative had become outdated and needed to change for her to progress at work.

Another example of this is how older people are viewed in the social discourse of media representation. Ageing is often portrayed through an 'age as decline' narrative (e.g. Thomas et al., 2014), which influences the declining value attribution to an individual through advancement in age. Add to this gender differences – whereby men are seen as wise and distinguished and older women are diminished in societal value (Sloane, 2023) – and there is an intersectional effect of age and gender, rendering women in mid- to later life as having reduced perceived work and societal value compared with workers of a younger age and their male contemporaries.

There is an inherently transitional nature to gendered ageing at work and this influences how identity work is conducted. However, how identity work is conducted is sometimes 'vague and underspecified' (Caza et al., 2018). There are many ways to draw on the broad literature and understanding of identity work to an exploration of experiences of ageing bodies at work. As ageing, or becoming older, appears to be a period of transition, I have focused on the literature around transitional identities (Caza et al., 2018; Ashforth & Schinoff, 2016; Beech, 2011; Alvesson et al., 2008; Beech, 2008). As such, this section begins with a presentation of how identity work interacts with liminality. Specifically, this book draws on the liminal identity work model (Beech, 2011) due to the transitional nature of ageing bodies at work.

2.2.2 *Identity work through the body*

Identity work is especially relevant to a period of transition (Beech, 2011; Ibarra, 1999). Identity work is conducted through physical appearance (Brown, 2015, citing Snow & Anderson, 1987), whereby physical or bodily identities are worked on to portray a desired sense of self or conform with others' perceptions of desired appearance (Caza et al., 2018). Identities are viewed through categorisations as those which are to be either embraced or resisted (Ybema et al., 2009), such as age and gender (or indeed the intersection of gender and age as a category). The embodied capital employed in or deriving from working harder might require new skills in performativity whereby workers must always be on and entuned to the social construction of how labour is valued at work. As Tulle and Krekula (2013) poetically put it, 'bodies become social – not inert shells for containing our souls – endowed with meaning . . . [and] intention'.

An emerging literature around gendered older worker identity has focused on experiences of gendered identity through the body (Hurd Clarke, 2018; Calasanti & King, 2018; Gray & Kish-Gephart, 2013; Riach & Cutcher, 2014) as the ageing body experiences physical changes throughout mid- to later life. Workers 'do age and gender' by managing their behaviour mindful of both category-specific ideals (i.e. age and gender) and of the potential need to explain the rationale of these behaviours (Calasanti & King, 2018). There exists polarised views on whether a woman should embrace an identity associated with her biological age or whether she 'should' strive to reduce the appearance of ageing; women seek feminine identity through use of hair dye, make-up, attire, diet and exercise, as well as body work (Hurd Clarke, 2010). Many of these 'shoulds' that are encountered by women in mid- to later life are arguably reinforced by unhelpful media representation perpetuating the 'age as declining value' narrative, which is unsympathetic to natural phases of ageing. Calasanti and King (2018, p. 15) found that their participants discussed having to work harder to maintain femininity through behavioural practices which would 'prevent them from appearing as if they had let themselves go'; however, the freedom of letting go can be 'liberating and personally satisfying', though can also be seen as 'unquestioningly accepting patriarchal gender norms' (Hurd Clarke, 2018).

2.2.3 *Identity work: motivations*

How individuals are perceived by others, to project an identity to others (Brown, 2001) or creating 'a body for others', can motivate how identity work is conducted (Cutcher & Achtel, 2017). Resolution of identity tension is the most common outcome of and motivation for identity work, most active and intense when identity is threatened or conflicted (Caza et al., 2018). However, identity work might not always result in a resolution, rendering the individual in an ongoing liminal state (Beech, 2011). A liminal state can be defined as being caught in between two aspects of self, for example old/not-old, whereby someone might chronologically be 50 and therefore be lumped into 'older worker' policy, but might not subjectively feel or act 'older'.

It has been argued that this liminal state could be drawn on as a form of resolution in itself (Beech et al., 2016). While a neo-liberal agenda suggests that identity work is an individual pursuit, relationships with significant others through social, domestic and organisational structures can equally provide support or undermine identity work of workers in mid- to later life as they transition through retirement decisions (Amabile, 2019) whereby being part of a community of women 'who got each other' can be a powerful coping tool in the transition of becoming 'older' (Butler, 2020). While it is generally accepted by identity scholars that identity work is relational (see Caza et al., 2018 for review), there are limited empirical studies on the specific role meaningful others play in an individuals' approach to and performance of identity work, in particular the power wielded by those others in relation to the individual (Winkler, 2018).

Identity work is engaged when self-identity in an otherwise stable context is disrupted, potentially triggering feelings of uncertainty, anxiety or self-doubt over the appearance of ageing (Cameron et al., 2019). The distinction between identity work and other concepts of organisational identity revolves around 'becoming, rather than being' (Alvesson et al., 2008). It is this transitional concept of becoming that speaks to the experience of the 'older worker', i.e. 'becoming' older, whereby identity work might be more salient through periods of 'radical transition' (Ibarra, 1999). Identity work then becomes a form of adaptive strategy, or coping.

Identity work could also be driven by aspirational identity (Beech et al., 2016; Alvesson & Robertson, 2006; Ibarra, 2015), whereby aspiration towards more legitimate forms of culture is conducted more by the middle classes and by women than any other group (Boyle & De Keere, 2019). For example, legitimation of identity construction relies on an 'appropriate identity' fit with both an individual's sense of self and with what a worker 'should' look and act like, given the organisational context (Swail & Marlow, 2018). This notion is supported by aesthetic labour literature revolving around the idea of what is an appropriate 'look' for the organisation (Warhurst et al., 2009). However, this raises the question of the feasibility of this congruence and the impact of potentially failing to associate one's work identity with what is desired – or simply put, 'getting it wrong'. Identity work does not always end in resolution, coherence or desired perceptions of others (Caza et al., 2018). The risk of unsuccessful identity work to conform is that individuals might 'lose the plot' of their identity (Thomas & Linstead, 2002) or breach implicit or explicit group rules, such as appearance norms, on what is accepted and expected (Langlois et al., 2000). However, I would challenge the extent to which complying and conforming drives the identity work conducted by women in mid- to later life due to the complexity of life at that stage of life.

2.2.4 Liminality: work identity transition

The term liminality derives from the Latin, *limen*, or threshold. For women in mid- to later life, this threshold presents a door into a new, unknown and possibly unwelcome space. Since its roots in anthropological studies around rites of passage, (Ibarra & Obodaru, 2016; Turner, 1969), liminality has been widely adopted in organisational literature to describe a period of transition – 'betwixt and between', which generally has negative associations (Beech, 2011; see Ibarra & Obodaru, 2016 for review of use in inter-disciplinary research). The conceptual development of liminality due to its recent popularity has a broader application than its original concept, with contemporary application challenging original assumptions, creating a 'modern-day liminality' (Ibarra & Obodaru, 2016, Appendix 1). It is interesting to note that the original model required 'elders and fellow liminars' or role models, and empathetic support, whereas the updated model relies more on a neo-liberal model of self-guided process, suggesting a lack of requirement or availability of adequate or accurate role models and 'self-made' support groups.

Little is known about the interactional relationship between individual and organisational identities whereby workers might find themselves in a liminal position referring to an intermediate state in which individuals are 'neither here nor there' (Turner, 1969), or 'betwixt and between' (Beech, 2011) as ordered by custom, law or convention (Terry, 2020). For workers in mid- to later life, liminality might result in finding oneself being offered membership of an 'older workforce', though not yet personally identifying with that label, i.e. older-not-old. Indeed, Ashforth and Schinoff (2016) referred to the liminal state being 'sense-breaking', where one does not possess a 'viable' identity for the target context. Heilman (1997) posited that 'stereotypes flourish in ambiguous performance settings', which is relevant to the liminal space occupied by the worker in mid- to later life who is unwilling to attach herself to the 'older' label. Further, Trethewey (1999) referred to an 'in between' state for female professionals with regard to how they felt societal and organisation pressures to present their bodies as 'masculine/feminine, sexual/asexual, revealing/hiding one's body'. This liminal embodied identity was presented as inherently negative and something of 'paramount concern for women in their professional lives'.

Terry's (2020) study of the liminal position occupied by mental health nurses found that occupational identity was seen by her participants as 'somewhere in the middle' as their roles were 'nuanced and complex' due to lack of role clarity. She agreed with Beech (2011) that a liminal sense is problematic and something to be resolved, which she suggested could be conducted through more clearly defined roles and an assertion to articulate them so that their contribution be recognised and understood. However, this assumes an element of agency and control, as did work on perceptions whereby individuals looking to ease pressure of non-conformity believed that they needed to uphold a false representation of themselves (Meister et al. 2014).

Meyer and Land (2006) had a more positive take on liminality: while in an unstable period of oscillation between identities, one can begin a journey of learning and self-improvement, as opposed to pre-liminars, whose development is stunted. This period of transition, whether it be viewed as positive or negative, may be a gradual dawning, or the realisation might arise suddenly from a catalyst, a 'turning point' (Brown, 2015) or 'triggering event', such as structural or cultural changes within an organisation (Beech, 2011) or emotional responses such as fear (Down & Reveley, 2009), embarrassment (Butler, 2020) and shame (Calasanti & Slevin, 2001). While continuing liminality, generally viewed as a negative position, might result in ongoing ambiguity and significant disruption to self, creating paradoxical identities (Beech, 2011), it could also be challenged as to whether workers in mid- to later life ever feel liminality or whether there actually is a transition to 'older worker'.

Model of liminal identity work

Beech's (2011) model of identity work draws upon a 'dialogic construction' of identity resulting in experimental, reflection, or recognition identity practices. Dialogic construction in this context simply refers to how individuals build a sense of self through talking with the self and with others. Experimental practices draw on an 'inside-out' discursive flow representing a paradoxical phase of liminal identity work, whereby contradictions of identity were experienced and individuals were compelled to resist temptations of an unwanted identity. This resonates with findings that female entrepreneurs pursue a legitimate work identity by experimenting with masculinised traits, which was highlighted as an outward-facing strategy, specifically focused on convincing external audiences of their viability and value at work (Swail & Marlow, 2018).

Reflection relates to change influenced by external sources or perceptions; it is how the construction of the self interacts with the world of work, culminating in coping mechanisms against stressful situations and strong pressures to accept the status quo (Beech, 2011). Recognition – characterised by anxiety, misalignment, tension and shock – is not simply a relabelling activity, but a new experience. This characterisation of recognition can be compared with challenges facing women in mid- to later life as they as they age, or 'become' older (Hurd Clarke, 2018).

Interestingly, it was recognition that acted as the start and the end of Beech's (2011) identity work cycle. Recognition relates to awareness of self within one's surrounds; for example, did you recognise something about yourself slowly over time (dawning), or was it a light-bulb moment (epiphany)? Recognition through external triggers (e.g. threat of redundancy) encouraged liminal identity work to adapt work identities to fit in with organisational culture and after experimental and reflection practices were conducted it was recognition that underlined the final liminal position. Petriglieri (2011) addressed this through 'identity threats', whereby this form of external trigger can be produced by the individual, by others or by societal norms, requiring an individual to reconcile the identity threat through protecting or restricting their identity. However, this process involved reducing the source of conflict, suggesting that the individual has the agency or power to do this.

This model is not alone in attempting to explain how individuals engage in identity work; indeed, recent research suggests that we currently have an 'unwieldy' understanding of identity work practices (Caza et al., 2018), but it provides a useful frame for this research into how women work by asking how they practise identity work through liminality, or 'in between' spaces, 'betwixt and between' identities, where they might be 'neither one thing or the other' (Turner, 1969, p. 96; Beech, 2011; Ibarra & Obodaru, 2016). What Beech's (2011) model did not sufficiently consider was the resolution of the identity work; his case studies displayed unresolved ambiguity, a disconnection and loss of social and organisation place. Indeed, in Beech et al. (2016), we see that resolution was not desired, where distinction and strength of identity was found in 'self-questioning'. While identity work has been reported as the path to 'coherent identities' (Brown, 2015, p. 27), or an attempt at reconciliation with transitions (Sveningsson & Alvesson, 2003), the liminar can become structurally invisible, occupying a paradoxical identity (Beech, 2011). Further, the model touches on perceptions, but not meta-perceptions, which are beliefs about how other people perceive the self, presenting an opportunity for comment and extension.

2.3 Influencing factors of work identity in mid- to later life

As demonstrated, the relationship that women in mid- to later life have with their ageing body at work appears to influence how they engage in identity work and how they experience liminality, the 'betwixt and between' of older-not-old. Looking more broadly to exploring the mechanisms (how) and influence of self or others (who) behind this relationship, studies suggest that a range of factors influence how women in mid- to later life engage in identity work through the liminal experience of their ageing bodies at work. These include: perceptions of self and others (Carter, 2016; Carlson et al., 2011; Meister et al., 2017), appearance bias (Langlois et al., 2000), successful ageing expectations (Zacher, 2015; Rowe & Kahn, 1997), the availability of role models (Ibarra, 1999) and individual differences of confidence (Griffiths et al., 2013; Caza et al., (2018), emotions (Winkler, 2018), age definitions (Riach & Loretto, 2009) and ageism or age discrimination, both overt and subtle (Loretto & White, 2006; Duncan & Loretto, 2004; Ng & Feldman,

2012). The literature review that follows explores each of these influencing factors as to how they work to influence older worker identity and attitudes as to how women in mid- to later life work.

2.3.1 Perception of self and others

How women in mid- to later life make sense of their ageing bodies at work is in part informed by how they are viewed and constructed not only by themselves, but also by broader constructions of gendered ageing bodies. Reflected appraisal (McMullin & Cairney, 2004) and meta-perceptions (Carlson et al., 2011; Meister et al., 2017) are our perception of how others view us through these social constructions. These constructs conceptually frame work identity, i.e. how a woman perceives that her identity of self is perceived by others in the world of work. What is unclear from these studies is how these aspects of perception of self and others affect not only worker identity but attitudes towards retention and extension of work. Further, these studies insufficiently critique the relational and emotional mechanisms behind these perceptions.

Ibarra's (1999) identity transition model of provisional selves requires a process of internal and external evaluation; however, she did not extend the range of feedback to meta-perceptions, drawing simply on 'external feedback' of meaningful others at work. Women in mid- to later life, more than men, differentiate between their internal and external selves, between their sense of self and their appearance to others (Hurd Clarke, 2018). As such, women in mid- to later life are more likely to experience a form of cognitive dissonance over their sense of identity at work, or disidentification (McMullin & Cairney, 2004; Gray & Kish-Gephart, 2013). Alvesson et al. (2008) referred to this dissonance as 'a mismatch between self-understandings and social ideals promoted through discourse', citing the mismatch as a grounding for identity work. However, studies have shown that this dissonance could be a positive distinction, such as internalised perceptions of others and projections of an idealised self, balance of similarity and belonging with uniqueness and individuation, or striving for 'optimal distinctiveness' (Beech, 2008; Brewer, 1991).

Whereas some individuals might readily self-identify as an 'older worker', reflected appraisal or meta-perceptions might result in personal disidentification because congruence with organisational and personal expectations are sought. Disconnecting from oneself with one's natural identity is an emotional activity, especially if the change(s) are forced upon an individual (Gray & Kish-Gephart, 2013; Cameron et al., 2019). This is potentially disruptive to self-esteem (McMullin & Cairney, 2004), leading to a disconnection between 'the inside and outside self' (Hurd, 1999; Hurd Clarke, 2010) and a disconnection with one's ageing body (Cameron et al., 2019), which can feel out of control (Steffan, 2021). Disidentification might also be borne by reaction to anxiety whereby discomfort is felt between members from different social groups (Gray & Kish-Gephart, 2013), supporting the influential role of out-group members (Roscigno et al., 2007). This concept of anxiety and fear was exposed by Shaw and Langman (2017) in their qualitative study of older adults (over-50s) in Australia, which they termed 'ageing anxiety' in relation to failing physical health. Further, Carter (2016) revealed that older female participants felt tension between strong neo-liberal accountability to be seen by others as healthily ageing and still 'needing' to be recognisable as feminine, which she coined as 'bodily anxiety'. This need for perceived femininity is interesting in light of self-desired masculinisation of the older female body at work to display equitable work performance (Swail & Marlow, 2018).

Anxiety around ageing might lead to identity anxiety, which is felt when a discrepancy or misalignment occurs between work identity and perceived 'professional image': the aim of identity processes and interpreting perceptions are to give a positive impression of oneself or to conform (Meister et al., 2014). Further, authenticity is experienced through self-awareness and relational orientation to others (Goldman & Kernis, 2002), which raises a question about the role of perceptions in seeking and feeling an authenticity of self. Acknowledgement of authenticity by meaningful others is important to individuals. Ibarra (2015) found that authenticity for many workers meant adhering to what is familiar or comfortable, whereby transitional identities specifically 'trigger a strong countervailing impulse to protect our identities'. Further, Ibarra (2015) asserted that viewing identities as works in progress enables an evolution of professional identity that provides a congruence between personal and organisational requirement, which suggests that authenticity ambition should satisfy not only the individual, but also the organisation. However, this creates a situation whereby the efforts borne by the individual is for the gain of both the individual and the organisation. In this case, the organisation gains without the associated cost of supporting identity work processes.

Meister et al. (2017) found identity asymmetries for women for whom gender was not important at work but who felt that it was important to meaningful others at work, thus making it an important part of their internal salience hierarchy. The authors concluded that identity work conducted requires the individual to have a 360-degree awareness of self and others, although I would question how many of us actually have this awareness. Further, Carlson et al. (2011) conducted a study of meta-perceptions investigating whether individuals understand the difference between how they view their own personality and how others view their personality. The authors found that in everyday interactions, individuals detected accurate distinctions between how they saw themselves and how others perceived them, further suggesting that an individual's self-perception was used as the basis of meta-perceptions.

Women, more than men, rely on perceptions of others in relation to appearance-contingent self-worth (Moya-Garofano & Moya, 2019), which can be a catalyst for internalising ageist assumptions (Amabile, 2019; Butler,

2020). This presents a problem as self-perception is often based on social constructions available to the individual and are open to misinterpretation (Hurd Clarke, 2018; Calasanti & King, 2018; Tulle & Krekula, 2013; McMullin & Cairney, 2004). Further, external perceptions are largely based on how we see ourselves to varying extents of accuracy and interpretation (Meister et al., 2014; Carlson et al., 2011; McMullin & Cairney, 2004). As such, a 360-degree awareness of self and others might be subject to misinterpretations and error of judgement. For clarity, this book draws on reflected appraisal and meta-perceptions concepts, grouping them together as 'perceptions of others', as separate constructs are beyond the scope of this analysis.

2.3.2 Appearance bias

We live in a social world where, like it or not, physical appearance matters and the body is central to worker identity (Nickson et al., 2016). We make fast, lasting assessment of others based on what we see and associated heuristics, which inform social judgements (Hamermesh, 2011; Heilman,1997, 1983; Hamermesh & Biddle, 1994; Heilman et al., 1988). Enquiry into appearance bias since the early 1980s has consistently provided evidence that 'attractive' people experience occupational advantages in recruitment and remuneration (Heilman, 1983; Webster & Driskell, 1983), promotion, predicted success and employment potential (Hamermesh, 2011; Langlois et al., 2000), and that they are seen as more co-operative and providing greater individual contribution at work (Andreoni & Petrie, 2008), even when controlling for cognitive skills, social background and occupational status (Anyzova & Mateju, 2018). Conversely, individuals perceived as 'unattractive' are more likely to experience adverse employment outcomes – including implications of professional incompetence (Heilman, 1997), lower trustworthiness and higher aggression (Krumhuber et al., 2007) – and can be seen as intimidating, unapproachable and a threat to others in the struggle for limited resources at work (Frevert & Walker, 2014). This could lead to what Petriglieri (2011) referred to as 'identity threat' whereby value, meanings or the freedom to enact an identity is compromised through perceptions and judgements of appearance.

Studies have since drawn on the 'beauty bias' to study appearance bias more broadly. Maestripieri et al.'s (2017) comprehensive essay on conflicting mechanisms behind appearance bias posited that evidence supporting the bias has been inconsistent and inconclusive, finding support for appearance bias through both the value of economic productivity (citing Barclay, 2017), and an evolutionary basis whereby labour is valued in line with evolutionary appeal of the worker (Buunk & Massar, 2014). An individual's value and investment in their own bodies as a source of labour in light of perceived economic value is a common thread in research on emotional and aesthetic labour, which is highly gendered (Warhurst & Nickson, 2007; Nickson, 2018). For example, men derive cultural capital from social and physical achievements, and women 'learn from an early age that they are prized for appearance' (Hurd Clarke, 2018).

Female workers, especially leaders and managers, feel pressure to invest additional resources including thought, time and effort into managing how others view them at work by developing coping mechanisms to navigate the experience of comparison with their male colleagues (Meister et al., 2017). Conversely, Borland and Leigh (2014) found no significant change in effects of appearance on household income for either men or women over time, suggesting that appearance advantages in younger adulthood translate to the same level (ranking) of advantage for workers in mid- to later life.

Moya-Garofano and Moya (2019) conducted experimental research on 263 younger adults, 140 of whom were women, testing aspects of self-objectification through personal body surveillance and comparison with appearance social norms. The authors also sought to distinguish individuals for whom appearance was important through a measure of 'appearance-contingent self-worth'. Women, not men, displayed a higher importance of appearance-contingent self-worth, which depended mainly on the perceptions of others. This finding highlights the role of gender, as well as the importance of perceptions of self and others; however, like many appearance-based studies, the authors did not consider workers in mid- to later life.

Findings of appearance bias at work and related perceptions suggest a complex structure in which gender and job and industry type play a role in how appearance bias manifests for individuals within different organisational contexts; however, the role of age and gendered ageing remains unclear. Practical implications of not challenging appearance bias at work risks perpetuating stereotypes based on appearance, especially when the decision-maker experiences a high cognitive load or time pressure, such as recruitment and management decisions (Johnson et al., 2010). In the context of current and future economic imperatives to encourage workers in mid- to later life to stay in or return to paid work (UK Parliament, 2023), employers and managers must better understand these underlying mechanisms of bias and discrimination.

2.3.2.1 Appearance-based judgements of women in mid- to later life

Appearance bias has been studied through mechanisms beyond the beauty bias, including weight (Nickson et al., 2016), attire (Howlett et al., 2015), grooming (Isopahkala-Bouret, 2017) and a gender-role congruity bias indicating the shielding effect of role seniority against appearance bias (Koch et al., 2015). To date, very few studies of appearance bias have considered mid- to later life participants. One exception is the work of Julia Twigg (2012, 2007, 2004), who suggested that certain aspects of appearance – in her case, gender- and age-related attire – appeared trivial to sociological and organisational scholars, as the masculine-defined world of work regards aspects of appearance as superficial. Further, Carter (2016) asserted that women are often characterised as trivial due to their concerns about appearance, despite the centrality of the body to a sense of self. How women display their bodies at work has significant and enduring employment consequences (Trethewey, 1999). Women in mid- to later life acknowledge that they are likely to be judged and excluded based the appearance of age and/or gendered ageism (Calasanti & King, 2018; Warhurst & Nickson, 2007; Sontag, 1979); however, the appearance of ageing can also result in workers in mid- to later life being seen and valued for their qualification and competence (Isopahkala-Bouret, 2017; Gray & Kish-Gephart, 2013), although this is likely to be the case for men more than women.

Appearance of bodily ageing is important here, as ageist assumptions which equate age and ageing with decline (Trethewey, 2000; Thomas et al., 2014) are inherent in the processes that marginalise workers in mid- to later life. Ill health is a significant 'push factor' in early exit from labour force participation (Winkelmann-Gleed, 2012) despite Ng and Feldman's (2012) much-cited meta-analysis, which found no relationship between age and general health problems. A consideration when editing this book was where to define limits of enquiry into 'health' of women in mid- to later life, which is a broad body of work in social and organisational gerontology. For the purposes of this discussion, health is positioned as physical health, rather than as mental health, except when there is a direct impact on the physical self (stress and anxiety). This decision was due to limited space and the original focus on the body, not due to any importance placed on one aspect of self over the other.

As chronological age increases, perception of physical health decreases (Loretto & White, 2006). While high self-rated physical health is a predictor of younger subjective age, which in turn is predictive of better health and longer life span (Kotter-Grühn et al., 2016), workers in mid- to later life experience relatively more decline as their resources naturally deplete due to chronological ageing (Kooij et al., 2011). Older unemployed workers are less likely than younger workers to regain employment, which can lead to adverse effects such as poorer physical health and decreased well-being (Edge et al., 2017). Further, workers in mid- to later life who retire from labour force participation early due to health conditions are more likely to face lasting financial disadvantage and a lower standard of living while at work and into retirement compared with healthy workers in mid- to later life who remain at work for longer (Schofield et al., 2015; Brown & Vickerstaff, 2011).

When general physical health is promoted through corporate culture, policy and values, 'being healthy' influences how individual employees are perceived, treated and evaluated at work (Powroznik, 2017). A form of healthism might emerge from these perceptions inferring that 'individuals have a social responsibility to achieve good health and those who do not are stigmatised for their unhealthy lifestyles and behaviours' and may face value-based judgements based on their 'unhealthy' appearance (Carter, 2016; Powroznik,

2017). Unintended consequences of prioritising looking healthy over being healthy for workers in mid- to later life include increased bodily anxiety, lowered self-esteem, unhealthy or age-inappropriate diet or exercise behaviours, and disidentification of self (Carter, 2016), potentially leading to internalised ageism.

A recent study into how older worker labour is valued through 'healthy ageing' provides insight into how physical health is just one part of a myriad of factors affecting workers in mid- to later life. Foweraker and Cutcher (2019) suggested that 'successful' or 'healthy' ageing is the ability to utilise embodied social capital for labour force participation, although this was gendered. Men in their study were in a privileged position, whereby they could draw upon the older worker aesthetic (where older equals wiser) through their accumulated social capital to achieve a sense of successful ageing, but this was not extended to female workers who faced discrimination based on their 'looks' (citing Ainsworth, 2002). As such, the women in their study were less likely to extract value from their ageing aesthetic as a form of capital and were more likely to face an expectation to make themselves look 'healthy and youthful'.

Similarly, successful ageing requires agentic behaviours, whereby individuals are encouraged – even expected – to cope with losses in subjective general health (Kooij et al., 2011) and to 'take care of themselves' with regard to health and have control over their ageing bodies (Truxillo et al., 2015; Carter, 2016). This is contrary to scholars who reject and rally against this form of neo-liberalism, calling for researchers to reject ideas of individualism which mask the role of agency or personal responsibility in a blame culture (Emirbayer & Johnson, 2008). As previously stated, this assumes that women have agency, where choice and control around health is actually constrained for many. The conclusion from the literature is that differentially for women, both health and appearance – or indeed, the appearance of health – are relevant to how women in mid-later life work.

2.3.2.2 The appearance of attire and grooming

Attire presents the naked body, which is central to experiences of ageing (Hurd Clarke, 2018), as the self to the social world (Twigg, 2007). Articles of clothing act as 'cultural mediators' which shape how experiences of ageing are 'imagined, experienced and performed at an embodied level' (Twigg, 2012). Attire is a 'situated body practice' based on everyday choices and self-presentation (Entwistle, 2000). And yet, attire and grooming of workers in mid- to later life has received very little attention in sociology and gerontology literature (Twigg, 2012) and even less in organisational literature, in which studies on corporate attire of all ages tends to ignore the role of the wearer (Peluchette & Karl, 2007).

As women are more likely to be judged by their appearance than men (Vaes et al., 2011), choice of attire can have a significant impact on impressions formed by colleagues being markers for sexualised gender (Howlett et al., 2015; Caven et al., 2013). For example, research has found that dressing only slightly more provocatively (above-the-knee skirt hem length and one extra button undone on a blouse) was detrimental to perceptions of intelligence for women in higher work positions (Howlett et al., 2015). Trethewey (1999) included attire in her study of embodied identities of professional women, finding that how bodies were dressed was associated with how bodies were sexualised and controlled by both the individual and meaningful others at work. Further, in their study on corporate attire, Peluchette and Karl (2007) found that the appropriateness of clothing was associated with employee self-perception of competence, trustworthiness (for formal attire) and friendliness (for casual attire); their study did not consider perception of others. Specifically, clothing that creates physical or psychological discomfort in the wearer has a negative impact on self-perceptions of productivity (Peluchette & Karl, 2007), causing concern for women in mid- to later life over dressing appropriately for their age as clothing is perceived as a 'cue of age' (Cameron et al., 2019).

Attire appears to engage its own dialogue or vernacular. Enabling successful engagement with the social world, and the world of work, is facilitated by 'being dressed correctly' (Entwistle, 2000), acknowledging a social desire that women in mid- to later life wear muted colours, or 'toning down' and 'adoption of self-effacing, don't-look-at-me clothes that reflect the imposed cultural invisibility of older people, particularly women' (Twigg, 2012). Attire monitors moral regulation (Twigg, 2012) and is narrated through moral nomenclature including 'good, bad, faultless, correct, vulgar, tarty, cheap' (Twigg, 2007, p. 295). It seems that personal responsibility of a healthy body extends to how it is dressed. Crawford (2006), in his study on the personal responsibility of the healthy body, aligned this way of thinking with adhering to a personal neo-liberalist moral compass of citizenship central to one's 'expression of self and individual responsibility'.

One example of moral regulation is through the old-fashioned yet widely-recognised term that directly addresses the intersection of gender and age as that of decline: 'mutton-dressed-as-lamb' (Twigg, 2007, p. 295). However, attire also provides women in mid- to later life with the opportunity for 'exploration of themes of resistance' balanced with the inclination towards conformity (Twigg, 2012). Isopahkala-Bouret (2017) found that appearance of bodily ageing, in their case grey hair, created an opportunity for older female workers to be seen and heard for their relevant skills and attributes, rather than through the lens of appearance bias, i.e. based on beauty or sexual appeal (Maestripieri et al., 2017). This line of thinking does not consider whether women want to be seen for their appearance, instead assuming a desired gender-neutral ageing body, which arguably works to marginalise women in mid- to later life.

Individuals face changing social roles throughout mid-life into later life, particularly relating to work and status change, which are associated with expectations of appropriate behaviour (Webster & Driskell, 1983; Magee et al., 2013; Cameron et al., 2019). As with health and menopause, how to dress the ageing body creates a paradox for the older female worker. On one hand, the older female is encouraged by society to dress and present her body appropriate to her age, shifting focus away from the sexualised body to the relevant skills and capabilities of the individual. However, we could argue that this assumes that the older female worker will readily accept this sexlessness, rendering her gender-neutral. Female workers in mid- to later life wishing to retain their femininity through embodied performance of the ageing body might risk being perceived as inappropriate, facing adverse reactions from others in the world of work, where their value is potentially precarious. This raises questions of who determines what is 'appropriate' and asks how is 'appropriate' communicated to and understood by working women? This can be addressed by considering the literature around successful ageing and role models, which follows.

2.3.3 'Successful ageing'[2]

So far, I have built a picture of how experiences of women in mid- to later life at work are contextual, represented by a myriad of factors including age, ageing, gender, occupational type and presentation of the biological and dressed body. Also identified was the expectation of neo-liberal attitudes towards successful ageing and managing one's own appearance of ageing at work (Cameron et al., 2019). Successful ageing describes a combination of healthy, active, harmonious and productive ageing (Carpentieri et al., 2016), whereby personal and social resources are co-ordinated to maximise well-being and it is generally described in terms of maintaining a positive balance between gains and losses (Baltes & Baltes, 1990; Freund, 2008).

Successful ageing, generally approached from a developmental life span perspective (Truxillo et al., 2015; Freund & Baltes, 2002), adopts neo-liberalism, whereby individuals are encouraged – even expected – to take care of themselves with regard to health and well-being, and whereby they are encouraged to remain actively engaged with society and work. This agentic behaviour extends to the ageing body. The neo-liberalist view of ageing encourages workers in mid- to later life to maintain or even mask the effects of ageing that might hinder their productivity in the workplace, presenting an image of the ideal older worker as someone who has not actually aged at all (Rowe & Kahn, 1997; Carter, 2016).

Foweraker and Cutcher (2019) suggest that successful ageing is the ability to utilise embodied social capital at work, although in their study, this was gendered. Men in their study were in a privileged position, whereby they could draw upon the older worker aesthetic through their accumulated social capital to achieve a sense of successful ageing, but this was not extended to female workers who face discrimination based on looks at much younger ages than men (Calasanti et al., 2013; Ainsworth, 2002). As such, the women in their study were less likely to extract value from their ageing aesthetic as a form of capital and are more likely to be expected to make themselves look healthy and youthful (citing Trethewey, 1999).

Despite its ubiquity, successful ageing is a poorly defined social construct (Zacher, 2015; Abraham & Hansson, 1995), and many scholars have called for a conceptual expansion of successful ageing (Rowe & Kahn, 2015) based on its narrative quality (Carpentieri et al., 2017). It can be argued that the comparative nature of successful ageing is flawed. People are deemed 'successful' if they score above the average downward trend of ageing (Zacher, 2015), suggesting that a perception of ageing is relative to peers or colleagues, where 'the attainment of goals can be measured against diverse standards and norms' (Baltes & Carstensen, 1996), creating an zero-sum environment (Strawbridge et al., 2002). This comparable ranking might reflect the cumulative beneficial effect of the resource-rich over the life span rather than the direct result of adaptive behaviours (Zacher, 2015; Freund, 2006). This book, therefore, draws upon the general theory of successful ageing, rather than specific measurement, demonstrating its utility within the language of identity work theory, while acknowledging its shortcomings as a theoretical tool for understanding the experiences of women in mid- to later life.

2.3.4 Role models of women in mid- to later life

The literature on the older body at work revolves around social normative expectations and perceptions (Cameron et al., 2019; Hurd Clarke, 2018; Caza et al., 2018; Warhurst et al., 2009). As individuals tend to seek role models who are older than themselves and individuals are expected to continue to naturally seek out role models (Gibson & Barron, 2003), this raises the question: who are the role models for this cohort of women in mid- to late life? What is not clear is how individual workers respond to draw upon inappropriate or unrealistic role models of women in mid- to later life, whereby role models have been identified as a fundamental tenet of transitional role identity (Ibarra, 1999) and less is known about how women in mid- to later life identify with role models, who their role models are and how role model identification impacts work outcomes (Gibson & Barron, 2003). Warhurst et al. (2009) posit that it is accepted that employers seek employees who are most appropriate to their organisational expectations, rejecting those who are less appropriate. Without peer-aged role models, it is unclear how any worker will understand what is 'most appropriate' to the organisation.

Ibarra (1999) wrote one of the seminal works on identity, presenting a transitional identity concept of provisional selves. As much of the subsequent work on identity formation was built on her early work, it is interesting to note the three foundational themes upon which her professional identity formation model was formed. Identity adaption requires the following with regard to potential identities: role modelling, experimentation and internal/

external evaluation. In fact, experimentation and evaluation are in part built on the primary concept of role modelling. Ibarra's iterative process of identity adaption requires individuals to identify with role models to whom they aspire and with whom they can connect and then rely on for feedback and guidance within the experimentation and evaluation phases. As the literature around workers in mid- to later life suggests, there is a paucity of appropriate role models, and where they do exist, they are often presented through a narrative of declining health, vulnerability and precarity (Thomas et al., 2014; Riach, 2007; Trethewey, 2000), which I argue is hardly aspirational. In fact, it could be suggested that for women in mid- to later life, role models are largely absent from the workplace due to the relatively low numbers of older female workers over 60 due to the recent change in the SPA and the comparatively few women in senior organisational roles (Meister et al., 2017; Brancu, 2023)

There is a seeming lack of role of models for workers in mid- to later life, especially women, where researchers have framed organisational role models through social comparison. Schilling (2015) for example, suggested that organisational cultures draw on social contexts for available role models, comparing with individuals from one's own social group to understand 'possible and desirable' work goals. This study also found that highly qualified women, who viewed themselves as gender 'pioneers', compared themselves with men of similar education and occupational status who had normative career trajectories. Schilling (2015) goes on to report that this between-gender comparison resulted in a 'hostile' working reality for many women including aspects of precarity, resulting in women avoiding career breaks and masking non-linear career trajectories. Her participants often worked long hours and recognised the need to align with a male model of working for advancement.

Similarly, Swail and Marlow (2018) found in their study on female entrepreneurs that their participants associated male role models with work success, emulating this through identity work by adopting masculine behaviours (e.g. acting hard and aggressive) as a pathway to legitimacy in their workplace, or modelling the norm. They also engaged in gender-deprecating language such as 'just two females' and actively acknowledging a process of masculinisation by 'encountering, observing and listening to men to pick up cues' about how to act and behave at work. The authors warned that by straying too far from their expected gendered performances individuals engaging in out-group identity work can damage personal legitimacy in the pursuit of organisational legitimacy. This study suggests that women sought role modelling from one source, i.e. from the masculine influences around them. However, it is thought that multiple developmental relationships or role models is a more effective method of professional identity development than focusing on one or a narrow group of individuals, or as Ibarra (1999) put it, 'one homogenous package'. It is this lean toward a heterogenous role model 'package' that speaks to Gibson and Barron's (2003) findings from their quantitative study that workers in mid- to later life tend to create 'composite role models' that helps them achieve their individual work goals. What is not clear from this study, or subsequent studies on older worker role models (Durbin & Tomlinson, 2014; Marcinkus Murphy, 2012; Sealy & Singh, 2010) is why workers in mid- to later life resorted to a composite role model. It could be suggested that this was due to the paucity of available and appropriate role models. Indeed, Sealy and Singh (2010) determined in their meta-analysis of role models and senior women's work identity development that better understanding of role modelling was needed to encourage successful work identity management for senior women. This was in part due to the lack of actual older role models, which was supported further by Durbin and Tomlinson (2014), who highlighted the lack of non-traditional career trajectory role models in their case female part-time workers.

2.3.5 The role of individual differences in identity work: confidence and emotions

Emotions are crucial to how individuals define themselves (Fineman, 2000; Stryker, 2004) and are 'a way of defining . . . one's place in a situation in terms of important values' (Gordon, 1989). As such, emotions present an individual within their organisational context in terms of their contribution and performative value. Fischer (1993) posited that emotions – guilt, shame, pride, anger – are controllable and are subject to personal rules, logic, moral values and ideals. Early theorists suggested that positive emotions can lead to a positively enhanced self-identity, whereas negative emotions can result in a threat to self-identity whereby 'emotion work' inherently becomes part of 'identity work' (Fineman, 2000).

More recent literature suggests that emotions are socially constituted, in that the social context within which the emotion is experienced is explicitly relevant or discussed (Kornberger & Brown, 2007) and in that they are socially constructed systems of discourse and practice (Coupland et al., 2008, Fineman, 2000, 2003). Emotions as discursive resources for identity work (Coupland et al., 2008; Marsh & Musson, 2008) are particularly salient when identity is threatened, leading to identity work to be done to resolve the identity conflict (Winkler, 2018). Further, emotional labour is conducted alongside aesthetic labour to seek value as an employee with one's organisation (Warhurst & Nickson, 2009). Emotions, therefore, as discursive resources, can be drawn upon to 'construct and maintain preferred versions of self' (Kuhn, 2009; Ahuja et al., 2019). However, emotions are thought to reduce identity work options and scope for individual agency through identity work (Clarke et al., 2009; Coupland et al., 2008). Paradoxically, then, if emotions shape worker identity and (re)produce particular forms of agency (Ahuja et al., 2019), what role do emotions play in how individual agency is conducted through identity work?

Winkler's (2018) review of the literature on emotions and identity work found that previous studies have approached the relationship between emotions and identity work in three ways. First, findings suggest that emotional experiences trigger identity work. Studies based on the precarious nature of self-identity (Beech, 2008, Sveningsson & Alvesson, 2003) suggest that work identity change and transition acts as a catalyst for negative emotions such as fear (Down & Reveley, 2009), insecurity of self (Alvesson & Wilmott, 2002; Beech et al., 2012), vulnerability or perceptions of 'losing the plot' (Thomas & Linstead, 2002), and anxiety (Ibarra & Petriglieri, 2007).

Second, Winkler (2018) posited that identity work is an emotional process. Identity work processes of defending and balancing work (role) identities was reported to result in negative emotions of vulnerability and stress (Beech et al., 2012). Identity work processes themselves can also trigger emotional responses such as fear, anxiety, doubt, frustration and loss, suggesting that overall, studies report a negative emotional response to identity work (Winkler, 2018).

Third, identity work can lead to emotional consequences of (un)successful identity work. As mentioned, the ultimate aim of identity work is a coherent identity of self and in relation to others (Caza et al., 2018). Successful identity work – that is, identity work that has achieved a sense of plausible and coherent identity – generally results in positive emotional outcomes such as happiness, relief and ease (Down & Reveley, 2009). Conversely, when identity work is unsuccessful in (re)establishing identity coherence, then negative emotions can ensue, such as frustration, shame and feelings of loss (Costas & Fleming, 2009).

Despite Beech's (2008) argument that emotions – specifically, emotional attachment – influence identity construction through a dialogic construction, or how individuals build a sense of self through talking with the self and with others, Winkler (2018) identified the lack of empirical studies that analyse the discourse of emotions as a catalyst for or behavioural tool in engaging in identity work. Indeed, Winkler (2018) reported that 'how emotions as discursive practice and bodily performance are linked to identity work' had not actually been reported in previous studies. Ahuja et al. (2019) also found evidence that negative and self-deprecating identity work was conducted to make sense of present work identities of young professionals. The authors found that 'emotion talk' through idealising, reframing and distancing of emotions as a discursive resource for identity work was used by junior professionals to present specific versions of themselves, relevant to the context. Their study challenged the assumption that identity work is used primarily to convey a positive sense of self (Brown, 2015) and found that negative emotions were adopted to render the present less important, instead focusing on a future work identity. They determined that emotion talk was used as a coping mechanism to deal with the mismatch between their ideal worker identity and their lived experience of work.

Caza et al. (2018, p. 904) found that individual difference, specifically confidence, is an under-explored area in identity work:

> those who are confident in who they are and feel like they can effectively make changes may be those who are more proactive in their identity work efforts, such as resisting control attempts or discarding others' perceptions.

Awareness of the precarious nature of emotions as triggers of identity work can influence an individual's confidence in the robustness of their identity (Winkler, 2018), an under-explored area of identity work research. There are few empirical studies on the relationship between confidence and identity work. One example was from Goretzki and Messner (2019), whose study of management accountants found that authenticity and confidence were related. Their participants' ability to engage in an authentic narrative enabled increased confidence in follow-up interaction with the client with whom they had the initial, positive and authentic interaction. However, ongoing work identity stability and coherence required ongoing affirmation and confirmation of work ability from the client. The authors also found that confidence was challenged when participants interpreted signals that their 'identity project' was not valued within the organisation. While referring to self-efficacy rather than confidence specifically, Meister et al. (2014) found that self-efficacy might influence how agency is harnessed to resolve a discrepancy between perceptions of one's own work identity and how others see us at work, which resonates with the broad interpretation of what 'value' actually means; for example, extracting value from an ageing aesthetic (Tre-thewey, 1999; Foweraker & Cutcher, 2019; Gray & Kish-Gephart, 2013; Isopahkala-Bouret, 2017; Warhurst & Nickson, 2007), conveying value from 'active ageing' (Riach & Loretto, 2009), 'healthy ageing' (Powroznik, 2017), the impact of value of personal identity (Alvesson et al., 2008), professional identity (Schein, 1975) and potentially compromising value through identity threats (Brown & Coupland, 2015; Petriglieri, 2011). Further, a lack of organisation and specifically collegial support contributed a threatened sense of confidence around work ability and value of labour at work.

2.3.6 *Age, but which age?*[3]

The majority of statistics reported, policies launched and empirical work conducted on the 'older worker' does so from a chronological age perspective, i.e. 50 years old in the UK (Age UK, 2020; ONS, 2016; Altmann, 2015). While over 50 is generally accepted as 'older' by policy-makers, this blanket definition has been described as problematic (Riach & Loretto, 2009). While chronological age is a useful temporal metric to understand an individual's position within the life span, there is a growing sense that researchers should look beyond chronological age to subjective age (Kotter-Grühn et al., 2016) as chronological age is no longer a 'unique reference point of the truth of ageing' (Tulle & Krekula, 2013).

Ryan et al. (2017) summarised alternative terms to older in their review paper of nurses: mature, experienced, seasoned, valuable. These subjective terms are inherently problematic; however, as their adoption in place of 'older' suggests their inaccuracy as descriptors for younger workers. Other approaches to subjective age in the study of work include felt age, look age and act age, where look and felt ages rarely align (Zacher, 2015). Riach and Loretto (2009) posited that 'active ageing' was a form of identity work to convey value and contribution of the older worker in unpaid work. One rationale for felt age is that feeling younger through individual resource mobilisation is correlated with the projection of good general health in older age (Armenta et al., 2017). The idiosyncrasy of subjective ageing is based on several constructs, including self-perception, older-age stereotyping, age identity and an awareness of age-related changes (Kotter-Grühn et al., 2016). Further, subjective ageing, in various metrics, is associated with the organisational concept of successful ageing (Zacher, 2015), which was presented in more detail earlier in this chapter. Duncan and Loretto (2004) took an interesting approach to defining age, finding that there was 'never the right age', evidenced by internalised ageism through employee perceptions, although it was unclear whether it was perceptions of self or others. For women in their study, 'never the right age' referred to negative attitudes of a woman's appearance of age or ageing, specifically finding a sexualised narrative and discourse around the female worker that was absent for men. While Duncan and Loretto's (2004) study is 20 years old, I posit that this sentiment remains valid in thinking about how women in mid- to later life engage with work through meta-perceptions of age and ageing.

Age and gender: discrimination, stereotyping and bias

This subsection briefly considers discrimination, stereotyping and bias as they relate to age and gender and crucially to the gendered ageing body. Discrimination, stereotyping and bias are terms that are often used interchangeably, but they have clear and distinct meanings (Koch et al., 2015). Discrimination is the prejudicial distinction and/or treatment of categories of people based on their membership to that category, whereby workers in mid- to later life can be an easy target for discrimination (Loretto & White, 2006) and women are more likely to experience gendered discrimination based on physical, bodily appearance and sexuality than men (Duncan & Loretto, 2004). Stereotyping is an evaluation made about individuals based on their membership of a demographic category. A stereotype is first activated through classification of an individual into a category – for example, women; the perceiver then applies the accepted stereotypes of that category, i.e. characteristics they associate with women, to form a basis of opinion about that person (Ng & Feldman, 2012; Bal et al., 2013). Stereotypes can result in bias (Koch et al., 2015). Bias is sometimes referred to as taste-based discrimination based on taste, preferences or prejudices (Maestripieri et al., 2017; Mobius & Rosenblat, 2006), and as such are inherently more subtle to detect and yet are no less impactful to the victim (Hosoda et al., 2003). Biases can be held against individuals who deviate from gender norms (Koch et al., 2015) – such as women in high-status 'male' sex-type jobs – and can have significant real-life consequences at work, including decisions around hiring, promotion and work allocation (Maestripieri et al., 2017, 2014).

Evidence suggests that employers view workers in mid- to later life as possessing many traits viewed as advantageous in the workforce: greater quantity and quality of experience and better interpersonal skills, and a perception that they are more committed, loyal and conscientious than younger workers (Loretto & White, 2006). Workers in mid- to later life show few age differences in performance and generally have more positive work attitudes than younger workers (Ng & Feldman, 2012). However, workers in mid- to later life might also be seen as less adaptable and less competent than younger workers (Gordon & Arvey, 2004). Duncan et al. (2000) found that young adults reported perceptions of performance decline in workers in mid- to later life and yet there was a general attitude that workers in mid- to later life should not be discriminated against, but equally they should not be afforded any special treatment, suggesting a form of 'age-blindness'. Ageing anxiety has been shown to affect one's own perceptions of ageing (Carter, 2016), and those who experience ageing anxiety themselves are more likely to stereotype based on age or avoid those of a similar age (Shaw & Langman, 2017).

Considering the amount of experience that workers in mid- to later life inherently bring to the workplace (Ryan et al., 2017), it seems counterintuitive that one's appearance of age would itself create a context in which the value associated with that age might not be respected. This could be explained by 'aesthetic labour' concepts, which are drawn upon by individuals to seek value within the world of work (Warhurst et al., 2009). Jyrkinen and McKie (2012) addressed this contradiction by suggesting that expectations of experience and knowledge are associated with older men, whereas women in mid- to later life – as young as 40 – do not carry the same expectation. Thus, organisational approaches to gender and age suffer inherent contradictions, potentially creating a vortex of missing knowledge and intellectual capital.

Subtle discrimination

Subtle discrimination is omnipresent in the contemporary workplace and can be more detrimental to an individual's attitude to work and organisational outcomes than overt discrimination (see Jones et al., 2016 for their meta-analysis on this subject). Subtle discrimination can occur with or without intention and may carry unconscious bias toward out-group members (Roscigno et al., 2007), reinforcing the argument that this is a bias mechanism rather than discrimination. It is this point on out-group members that is potentially salient for workers in mid- to later life due to the persistence of age stereotypes (Ng & Feldman, 2012), raising questions about the influence of out-group members – or in the case of workers in mid- to later life, the influence of younger others.

Jones et al. (2017) posited that the target individual is often left at a disadvantage due to the ambiguous nature and subtlety of the discriminatory act, be it banter, eye contact, informal exclusion or job allocation. Subtle discrimination is so pervasive at work that it is very difficult to attribute it to a protected characteristic or whether the discriminatory behaviour resulted for another reason such as personal bias, suggesting that subtle discrimination can be identified and controlled with increased awareness, stigma acknowledgement and increased salient information about the target. However, Hosoda et al. (2003) found that more relevant and positive information on the target did not positively addresses bias and stereotyping on appearance-based judgements, as it was shown to do to other forms of bias and discrimination. This suggests that appearance-based judgements, or appearance bias, and associated discrimination – both subtle and overt – are particularly enduring and pervasive.

Hurd Clarke (2018) offered an interesting example of age-related subtle discrimination through the acceptability of appearance bias of older people: greeting cards. It is common to find greeting cards using physical signs of ageing (wrinkles, stoop, bodily sagging, incontinence, erectile dysfunction), though the inherent prejudice and bias is rarely challenged: it is seen as humour despite reinforcing a harmful stereotype of gendered ageing. Sontag (1979) referred to the appearance of wrinkles, grey hair and sagging skin as the double standard of ageing that judges women based on appearance more harshly than men. It appears that, for many, it is socially acceptable to openly and actively stereotype older people, especially women, based on the appearance of gendered bodily ageing when other minority groups are protected.

In conclusion, how women in mid- to later life work has been largely absent from studies on the workplace, which is surprising considering the centrality of gendered ageism to a workers' sense of identity (Carter, 2016; Calasanti & King, 2018), their productivity, feelings of discrimination (Bal et al., 2013) and the ubiquitous nature of the performativity of and through the body. The mid- to later life course phase is a period of change for women at work. As such, the theoretical concepts of liminality (Ibarra & Obodaru, 2016) and the dialogic construction of liminal identity work (Beech, 2011) allows us to consider how women in mid- to later life navigate the transitional nature of becoming 'older' while maintaining their place and their identity at work. Further, successful identity work requires a 360-degree awareness of self and others (Meister et al., 2017), which is why meta-perceptions are so important to consider as part of work identity and identity work. So, too, is awareness of how women in mid- to later life internalise or shield themselves against (gendered) ageism. Further, the assumed agentic nature of identity work resonates with the management literature around successful ageing (Zacher, 2015), and yet these bodies of work are rarely combined (Foweraker & Cutcher, 2019).

This literature review has highlighted that women in mid- to later life, through experiences of their ageing at work, may encounter barriers to retention and extension of work. Barriers include ageing as decline not fitting with desired labour productivity (Riach et al., 2015), and workers are expected to present as healthily ageing through socially responsible behaviours, coping with perceptions of healthism, whereby health is the main barrier to working longer (Edge et al., 2017); and internalised ageism through the appearance bias mechanisms of aesthetic and productive labour (Langlois et al., 2000; Warhurst et al., 2009). Taken together, these barriers create a focus for women in mid- to later life to agentically and individually manage their performance at work through the influence of meta-perceptions (Carlson et al., 2011; Hurd Clarke, 2018) and through internal and external evaluation of identity discourses (Ibarra, 1999) – a reminder that a focus on the woman to enable herself for work insufficiently places focus on the employer to support the health and well-being needs for women in mid- to later life.

This literature review had two key objectives; first, to present a rationale for the timeliness and relevance of an exploration into factors affecting how women in mid- to later life work; second, to explore how distinct theories and concepts might work together to better understand experiences of gendered bodily ageing at work and its affect on continued labour force participation. To summarise, three core concepts of the ageing body at work, identity work and liminality comprise the core theoretical framework of this book, supported by influencing factors of older worker identity. The following chapter of this book presents the method and methodology adopted to address the research objective and questions of Study 1 and to explore how women in mid- to later life work.

Notes

1 The term 'successful ageing' is widely used in academic writing; however, I am reluctant to use this term without critique, as it is a value-laden label in its own right. I am uncomfortable with the term as where there is success, there is also failure, and ageing is not a zero-sum game. There is also the question of what does 'success' in ageing actually look and feel like, and the matter of through whose eyes this success is valued. This is an important critique of any investigation and writing on value within the workplace. Further, the body of literature around successful ageing focuses on choice, control and agency when the reality for many women in mid- to later life is that their paths are constrained within boundaries over which they have little choice and control. As such, the term is adopted in this book due to its relevance to the field, but please note that it is not without due critique.

2 I will admit to not be a huge personal fan of this term, as where there is success, there is also failure, and I'm not sure that is particularly helpful narrative around ageing. In the interest of research objectivity, however, I use the term as it was intended, as it can be a useful construct for understanding how people use adaptive strategies as they age.

3 I use the term 'mid- to later life' throughout this book. Study 1 relates to women over 50 and Study 2 relates to women over 40. Mid- to later life is a term that appears to elicit a relatively positive or neutral response as opposed to 'older worker', or 'later life', or even 'over-50s', which can be open to criticism around a focus on chronological age.

3 Research methods

In this chapter, I explain the methods adopted for my research. I start this chapter by demonstrating the rationale behind certain methodological choices of research planning and design, participant recruitment, data collection and analysis. These processes worked to evolve the research objective and questions stated in the previous chapter. Study 1 is a small(ish) exploratory qualitative study consisting of semi-structured interviews. It is a perfect place to start when exploring a theory or an area for which there has been little research evidence provided. Study 2 is less exploratory as the themes from Study 1 informed what questions I was asking; as such, Study 2 was set up as a survey and could reach out to more participants, as it was not as in-depth as interviews. This chapter was written to provide a detailed approach to support those who plan to conduct an exploratory study such as Study 1. I often receive emails asking for examples of the tools that I use during these studies, so I have provided these in the appendices. Much more is published on survey and quantitative studies so I have not replicated these works in this book.

3.1 Research planning and design: Study 1

3.1.1 Development of research ontology and epistemology

Research for Study 1 was conducted over a three-year period from September 2017 to September 2020. I spent much of this first year deciding on which ontology and epistemology to adopt to develop my research questions (both terms are explained in this chapter). I knew that I wanted to better understand 'factors affecting labour force participation of workers in mid- to later life', as I suspected then that this would be an increasingly important issue for workplaces and government policy, which turned out to be true.

I drew on methodological (Huff, 2009) and empirical (Bowman et al., 2016) sources to help me form a theoretical framework within which I could inductively work towards a study of gendered ageing at work. Inductive in this context simply means an approach of data analysis that is looking for themes made through researcher interpretation. Gioia et al. (2012) argued

DOI: 10.4324/9781003439257-3

that 'the single most profound recognition in social and organisational study' is that we make sense of our experiences and what we see through social constructions, which requires a focus on the individuals and how they construct and understand through experiences. For this reason, this book's primary level of enquiry is the individual and the secondary level of enquiry is the individual worker's interaction with their specific organisational factors.

Social constructionism accepts that there is an objective reality and is concerned with how knowledge is constructed and understood, as such is epistemological and makes no ontological claims (Berger & Luckmann, 1991). From this viewpoint, I focused on articulating an epistemology of how knowledge is constructed. Knowledge cannot be separated from the knower (Alvesson & Skoldberg, 2000) – or as Gioia et al. (2012) put it, 'advances in knowledge that are too strongly rooted in what we already know delimit what we can know'. As such, a social constructionist epistemological approach was taken to collect and analyse data that support this book on how women work in mid- to later life.

As stated, the level of analysis of this book, or how I planned to construct knowledge, is primarily the individual – crucially the individual narrative of identity, driven by social and organisational contexts (Bowman et al., 2016). As such, it is the participant's perception of self, constructed within these contexts, that is relevant here. Brown (2001) highlighted the importance of personal narrative in understanding oneself. To that end, the research design employed open-ended questions to guide the interviews. Interviews considered the importance of the cumulative effect of experiences, changes and adaptions to the world of work. It then followed that participants were asked how their work had changed over the course of their life, which prompted a comparison of being a younger and 'older' worker.

Ontology can be described as the science or study of being (Blaikie, 2018), or simply put, what is being studied. For example, Tulle (2008) called for a new ontology of ageing, specifically a new approach to studying the subject of ageing bodies. In this case, if the 'what' or the subject is the ageing body, then we should consider what role epistemology plays in that question. To answer this, we can note that two important aspects of ontology are objectivism and subjectivism. Objectivism 'is an ontological position that asserts that social phenomena and their meanings have an existence that is independent of social actors' (Bryman, 2012), whereas subjectivism perceives that social phenomena are based on perceptions and fits with our interpretation of constructionism.

A social constructionist epistemology lends itself to qualitative data and analysis (Huff, 2009). Taylor et al. (2016) highlight that quantitative approaches inadequately attribute meaning to the complex and sometimes paradoxical experiences of workers in mid- to later life, whereas qualitative research is capable of providing a more nuanced approach to individual experience, addressing the highlighted lack of individual focus on workers within specific and unique employment contexts (Loretto & Vickerstaff, 2013).

Amabile (2019) in her methodological paper on understanding retirement stories suggested that researchers should adopt qualitative research to seek out common patterns in experience and transitions with high individual differences in 'financially secure people who are demographically quite similar'.

There remains a preponderance of quantitative work into factors affecting labour force participation of workers in mid- to later life. Specifically, there exists a paucity of qualitative research that has sought to gain insight into the thoughts, opinions and experiences of ageing individuals themselves (Taylor et al., 2016). However, there have been a number of studies that have set the stage for qualitative work in this area. Early work by Loretto and White (2006) employed a qualitative approach to explore the 'complicated interplay between attitudes, practices and policies', which the authors felt enabled them to 'capture detail beyond the capacity of quantitative methods'. Since then, qualitative studies have sought to understand experiences of workers in mid- to later life more deeply by providing an audience to 'missing voices' on perceptions of ageing (Martinson & Berridge, 2015). Narrative is particularly salient to workers in mid- to later life who strive to maintain a 'good strong story' (Carpentieri & Elliott, 2014), whereby there is value in simply providing a platform for workers in mid- to later life to retell experiences.

3.1.2 Participant recruitment

Participants for the first phase of pilot interviews were recruited through word of mouth. Participants were recruited through response to flyers that I sent out to employers within Edinburgh, where I had a named contact. Individuals then contacted me directly subsequent to their employer recommendation. Participants were also recruited through snowballing from interview 12, at which point some participants actively contacted me through word of mouth as they desired a platform to discuss their personal issues around ageing at work, specifically around menopause. The research was conducted in Edinburgh within a UK context due to convenience. In general, recruitment was relatively straightforward; however, I was challenged by one participant who suggested that by my use of the term 'older worker' in the title of my recruitment literature, it had rubbed 'feathers the wrong way . . . I thought older was someone over 60'. This prompted my questioning of the seemingly arbitrary age of 50 as 'older'.

The reason Study 1 draws on participants over 50 years of age as 'older' falls into two categories: government policy and academic literature around workers in mid- to later life. There is also the consideration of the social construction of 'older', which I have already addressed more broadly in the literature review. In the UK, it is generally accepted that 50 years of age is the chronological threshold whereby one 'becomes' an older worker. This is not due to age discrimination legislation, which does not protect any specific age in the UK, but is more a reflection of government initiatives and industry norms. For example, products such as life insurance (e.g. aviva.co.uk), lifestyle (e.g. silversurfers.com) and sport/leisure (e.g. saga.com) apply the chronologically arbitrary age of 50 as the entry point for their services. Similarly, Age Scotland, Scotland's national charity for supporting 'older people', also state on their website that they support the over-50s (ageuk.org.uk/Scotland).

Fifty as 'older' is adopted as the academic norm by many active researchers in organisational and psychology studies (Zacher, 2015, 2013; Rudolph, 2016). Note that there are country differences; for example, Australian studies and researchers adopt 45 years of age, a reflection of age discrimination legislation. There is a movement in quantitative life course analysis to move away from using chronological age due to its perception as an 'empty variable' in that it insufficiently reflects within-person changes over time. While Bohlmann et al. (2018) argue that chronological age remains an important temporal metric for mapping individual differences and employment outcomes within the working life span. Other 'ages' have been suggested by quantitative researchers, including biological age, psychological age, social age and organisational age, supporting Baltes' (1997) life span perspective that ageing is a 'multi-dimensional and multi-directional' process.

People perform their age constantly, but they also give meaning to other ages, ageing and to age in general through the performativity of being older (Calasanti & King, 2018). This book acknowledges the role of chronological age, whereby 50 years acts as an established structural marker of older for government and organisations, but instead of the term 'older', I defer to 'mid- to later life'. Similarly, I refer to aspects of subjective age as a number which supports or contradicts one's chronological age (Kotter-Grühn et al., 2016). Further, the term 'ageing' is used to describe the temporal and transitional nature of the biological and socially constructed body (Hurd Clarke, 2010), but of course we are all ageing. Similarly, the term 'gendered ageing' is to determine difference between how women experience and perform age; not as that which is 'done' to women (Steffan, 2021).

I posit that this research would not be greatly enhanced by a flexible definition of workers in mid- to later life, and yet I do not agree that turning 50 equals 'older'. I address this conundrum further in the data and discussion chapters reflecting on how participants reacted to turning 50 or being labelled as 'older'. As further defence of this issue is beyond the scope of this book, I have relented to adopt the somewhat arbitrary chronological age of 50 years for participant selection, data collection and analysis. One interesting point to address was from a participant in this study who thought that using 50 to describe older was 'a negative thing' and that older worker 'was an academic term that is now out of sync with actually how we live and work'.

3.1.2.1 How many participants?

The golden rule of participant numbers seems to be stop when 'saturation' is reached; however, I found myself questioning the meaning of the word saturation. Saunders and Townsend (2016) gave an interesting answer to this question as a balance between depth and breadth: 'justification for the number of participants appears to be based on transparency, showing that data collected are of sufficient depth to provide salient information in relation to research purpose and of sufficient breadth to allow coverage within the responses'. The authors then go on to analyse 244 articles, 91% of which used one-to-one qualitative interviews. They found that within organisation studies journals, the median number of participants in both top tier journals (example given: *Human Relations*) and mid-tier journals (example given: *Organization*) was 30 interview participants.

Further, a glimmer of what might have been 'saturation' arose at my 20th interview when codes started to present multiple participants and I started hearing the same phrases and words repeated by participants. However, I cannot help but wonder how saturation could ever be reached when each person's personal narrative around their identity is unique. I decided to stop interviewing at 26 participants and start analysing data, only to conduct further interviews if approached by a potential participant. In the end, data presented in this study reflect 28 participants, seven of whom are men and are not included in this book due to its focus on the experiences of women. Further, this is a book about women, as all participants identified as cis-gender (Table 3.1).

3.1.3 Participant sample characteristics

The sample in this book consists of 21 women ranging in age from 47–62 years (see Table 3.1). (Note that Harriet approached me after a recommendation from another participant and asked to be interviewed, which I accepted despite her age being below 50 years.) Fourteen participants were married, four divorced, two single and one widowed. Only four participants had no children. The sample was relatively well educated, with 14 participants stating a university education. A high proportion of the sample worked in the education sector, albeit not all participants were teachers within these industries. There was a broad range of income and financial preparedness for retirement; for example the personal income range was from £11,000 annual gross salary to well into six figures. Similarly, household income offered a broad range, which was indicative of the diversity in marital status and an important reminder why household information is also important when looking at how individuals engage with paid work; arguably, this is especially the case when studying women's workplace participation.

3.2 Materials and procedure

3.2.1 Life history research

Due to the age of the participants, there was an inevitability of life history being a part of the study, but it was unclear to what extent to foreground or

Table 3.1 Participant characteristics – Study 1

Participant (pseudonym)	*Age*	*Children*	*Education*	*Marital status*	*Job*
Harriet	47	1	Tertiary	Married	Director
Adele	50	3	Tertiary	Married	Doctor
Julia	50	0	Tertiary	Married	Teacher
Laura	50	2	Tertiary	Single	Teacher
Rachel	50	1	Tertiary	Married	Lawyer
Tania	50	2	Tertiary	Married	Academic
Ursula	50	0	Vocational	Married	Administrator
Catherine	51	2	Tertiary	Married	Counsellor
Penny	51	2	Tertiary	Married	Teacher
Bronwyn	52	3	Tertiary	Divorced	Doctor
Stella	52	2	Tertiary	Married	Teacher
Deborah	53	3	Tertiary	Married	Counsellor
Monica	53	2	Tertiary	Married	Nursery Nurse
Georgina	55	3	Tertiary	Married	Director
Fran	56	0	Secondary	Divorced	Administrator
Vera	56	0	Tertiary	Single	Events Manager
Isla	58	2	Secondary	Widowed	Project Manager
Natalie	60	2	Vocational	Married	Administrator
Evelyn	61	2	Secondary	Divorced	Receptionist
Kara	62	2	Vocational	Divorced	Secretary
Orla	62	2	Secondary	Married	Nursery Nurse

Note: No participants identified as anything other than cis-gender, and therefore biological sex is female and gender is described as woman/women for all participants in Study 1

background the cumulative (dis)advantages gained over the life course. Life history research considers identity, authenticity and truth of lived experience; interrogates lives in context, relevant to age and ageing; and seeks to make sense of life as a complex mix of individual narrative and experiences (Tulle, 2008). Tulle asserted that research can be conducted to challenge existing ontologies; indeed, she called for a new ontology which 'does not trap older people in the dichotomy of bodily decline or disembodied selves'. This book follows this call to constitute a new ontology of ageing, or a revised or clarified concept of what is being studied.

3.2.1.1 Life grids

I came to the life grid method through conversations with colleagues who had had varying levels of success with them as a method of data collection, as well as from the relatively few organisational studies that draw on life grids. For example, Taylor et al. (2016) encourage the use of a life course perspective to challenge outdated age stereotypes and the 'stereotypical and outdated male model of continuous labour market participation across the life course'. Further, Parry et al. (1999) called for more research and publications of the combination of life grids with semi-structured interviews. However, Nico (2016) found that few researchers took up this call and few studies have either applied this method or written about it, attributing the paucity of empirical studies drawing on life grids to qualitative and quantitative researchers reluctant to find a hybrid method.

The life grid originated as an instrument of the quantitative researcher to research longitudinal data (Nico, 2016) and was traditionally presented as columns for life spheres and rows as time (Blane, 1996; Parry et al., 1999), designed to present individual life course trajectories; a format which I adopted in my life grid design (see Appendix 2 for image). Using life grids alongside semi-structured interviews allowed for life course events to be displayed with the flexibility of a non-linear narrative.

Nico (2016) also found that the life grid acted to aid the participant's memory of relationships between events; indeed, Berney and Blane (1997) referred to the life grid as an aide-memoire in their data collection, and Parry et al.'s (1999) study on smoking drew on the life grid to study life course patterns of smokers in later life. The life grid was presented as the tool to overcome one of the most criticised elements of qualitative academic rigour: that of memory distortion of retrospective data collection (Nico, 2016) whereby the life grid could 'release detail from memory by juxtaposing different information from the same period of life' (Blane, 1996). The life grid could partially address Bourdieu's (1990) warning about life course research, or his 'biographical illusion', which is simply a form of memory distortion engaged by the participant, enacted through the interview process, enabled by the interviewer.

> The narrative, whether biographical or autobiographical . . . the discourse of the interviewee who 'opens up' to an interviewer, offers events which may not all or always unfold in their strict chronological succession.
>
> (Bourdieu, 1977)

I found both positive and negative method aspects of using a life grid method. First, the positive. In keeping with Nico (2016), the life grid format not only gave structure to the interview, but worked to stimulate participants' connections between life events, or as Nico (2016) put it: 'at no other moment in their lives will the interviewees be in a position to visualise a map of their real lives with their paths duly recorded':

> How old was I? It was about 10 years ago, (long pause) probably around the time that my exercise routine changed. I never really connected that (pause) there you go. Um (long pause) and also the menopause has been quite challenging for me to be perfectly honest with you.
>
> (Fran, 56)

Also positive, the life grid offered a shared project to work on and develop throughout the interview. Indeed, Adele, a 50-year-old doctor and professor, found using the life grid very 'helpful' as an interview focal point and as an aide-memoire:

Participant: I think this is a great idea. Because it gives someone something to look at, so I'm not just [long pause and looks up at me] . . . .

Interviewer: Staring at me the whole time?

P: [staring at you the whole time] [laughs] which feels a little bit [long pause] when you're talking about something quite personal, so that could be a little too close, and helps you think about things and it gives you something to keep focused on, so I think that's very helpful.

I: The idea is to help you get your timeline sorted.

P: [That's right], it jogged my memory, bizarrely, or I felt it relevant to say something about my [content], which has been, when I think about it, I see this [long pause – points to life grid] I realise it has been quite a big part of my life bizarrely.

While I understand the conceptual and procedural benefits of the life grid as a method of data collection, as detailed in the preceding conversation, few papers on life grids have critiqued their use. As such, I offer my own critique here. The life grid format encouraged some participants to discuss elements of their history that were not as relevant to even the broadest interpretation of ageing at work. It was noted that even at this early stage I was, as the researcher, making a judgement on what was 'relevant' (see field notes from Evelyn's interview which follows). It was this balance that I found challenging. The life grid offered participants tangential narrative paths: an opened door which proved difficult to close.

The following summary outlines negative aspects of my experience of using the life grid method:

1. Life grids need more time than semi-structured interviews (Adele, for example, only booked an hour on her parking meter).
2. It encourages greater focus on historical events and subsequent life course trajectory, when perhaps a participant does not want to 'look back' (Penny: '. . . you just live your day, don't you? It's hard when you have to look back and analyse.')
3. Participants can go off on a tangent (I have provided my field notes which elaborate on Evelyn's story which follows).

Researcher field notes: Evelyn, 61, receptionist, was quite a challenging interview. She turned up 20 minutes late, looking quite stressed. It was a very hot day, 25 degrees. She looked very hot, sweaty and red in the face, so I gave her water and a cup of tea and 10 minutes just to relax a bit. She looked very on edge and stressed. She smiled very rarely throughout the interview. She was very keen to be interviewed, having voluntarily contacted me to participate, but I had the impression that she was just unsettled from the start. She used the life grid as a mechanism to discuss her broader family issues of troubles and internal disputes between her children. I was not quite sure how far to go into her family history. I made the decision to move on from that line of narrative, but the life grid gave her cause to return to her broader family story.

Overall, the life grid provided a useful method with which to collect life course data. However, as I have detailed, the method is not without its challenges which researchers should consider before adoption.

3.2.1.2 Topic guide: semi-structured interviews

Qualitative research allows marginalised and socially invisible groups to have their voices heard (Nico, 2016), and it is the responsibility of the researcher to ensure a faithful representation of their experiences. To that end, I adopted the role of storyteller rather than spokesperson or social activist. As discussed earlier, Nico (2016) suggested that Bourdieu's (1977) biographical illusion is an ally of researcher-as-spokesperson for minorities whereby an excessive formalisation of methods can lead to excessively descriptive analysis. As such, I used a flexible approach to question type, which was based on a normative flow of the conversation. Closed questions were employed to obtain demographic data and were avoided in the main interview in favour of open-ended questions and, when appropriate, probing questions, such as 'how so?' or 'can you tell me more about . . . ?'. Reflective questions were adopted to encourage further disclosure of emotions or feelings, although this was performed carefully and with caution – always with the well-being of the participant in mind. See Appendix 2 for the topic guide used in Study 1.

3.2.1.3 Part A: demographic information

I collected information on age, marital status, height, weight and personal and household income. Much of the demographic information collected was motivated by the initial literature review, which focused on appearance bias.

Also motivated by literature around well-being at work, I collected data on job satisfaction and self-rated health (SRH). SRH is a widely used indicator of overall health used in labour supply equations (Kalwij & Vermeulen, 2008; Armenta et al., 2017); as such, I decided to gain a sense of overall health on a Likert scale of 1–5. The majority (82%) of participants rated their SRH as 4 or 5, which is defined as 'good self-reported health' despite some participants reporting serious health complaints. This supports Kalwij and Vermeulen's (2008) study, in which 73% of their sample of over-50s reported a 'good self-rated health' and further they found that self-reported health and objective health indicators were highly correlated. It was the effects of menopause, specifically energy deficits, which seemed to have the biggest impact on reduced SRH for women in this study.

I believed that some participants were surprised by this level of data collection as they were attending an interview, but it was important to understand individual aspects of the participant and their life course, which was explained to participants. Nico (2016) states that 'qualitative researchers should not be shy in trying to collect other information about the individual, even if this information apparently contradicts or obscures the version of events narrated by the interviewee'. This demographic information was collected at the beginning of each interview. On reflection, the collection of these data did not adversely affect the interview and actually acted as a form of ice-breaker; given the opportunity, I would repeat the order, content and method of collection.

3.2.1.4 Part B: open questions

Open questions allow qualitative research to 'identify factors that might lead to different outcomes from seemingly similar starting points' (Amabile, 2019). The topic guide (see Appendix 2) listed five open questions, which were asked of all participants. These questions are as follows:

1 Can you tell me about your job and what it entails on a weekly basis?

   This question was designed to gain an understanding of the organisational context in which the individual was employed.

2 Can you describe how your work has changed during your life?

   This question was designed to capture the life course aspect of changing nature of work for the individual within structural and external organisational and broader societal factors.

3 What does the term 'successful ageing' mean to you personally? How does it relate to your work?

   This question was motivated by extensive recent work within organisational studies by Zacher (2015), following from earlier work by Baltes et al. (1999), whereby the term 'successful ageing' is ubiquitously adopted for studies on and around ageing. I wanted to gauge a reaction to this term rather than simply adopt it within the study. It was my sense that, despite its prevalence in organisation and psychology studies, the term 'successful' is subjective and somewhat loaded. To the best of my knowledge, no study has asked for a participant reaction to this academic term from the individuals for whom it is used to critically understand.

4 Is appearance important to you?

I asked this question to focus on experiences of appearance bias and appearance of bodily ageing, placing experiences of the individual as the line of investigation. Bodies are gendered objects leading to an expectation of bodily appearance based on group membership (Calasanti & King, 2018), and appearance is an important aspect of older worker's experiences of ageism in the workplace (Hurd Clarke & Griffin, 2008; Krekula, 2016). Specifically, I asked, 'Is appearance important to you?' – not 'Is your appearance important to you?' which was then open to participant interpretation.

5 Do you think that your appearance is important to others (at work?)

This follow-up question moved the focus of the previous question to more structural aspects of work. This question sought to investigate whether an appearance and perception ontology, which is generally based on younger workers, applies to workers in mid- to later life.

3.2.1.5 Part C: direct questioning, or the value of conducting a pilot study

This question was used in the pilot phase only. The initial topic guide included direct questions on appearance bias, such as, 'Have you ever been treated differently at work based on appearance?', which I removed for the main study, as I felt on retrospection that this was too leading. It also had the effect of participants offering an immediate 'No' in response, as it was either too confrontational or perhaps it was too direct a question and perhaps one they had insufficiently considered. The topic guide for stage one also included the question, 'How do you approach getting ready for work in the morning?'. This question was designed to focus the participant on aspects of appearance, but it did not really work as one participant gave the impression that it was a bit superfluous and another used it as a conduit to talk about motherhood. Ultimately, I did not draw on this section of the topic guide in the main study.

3.2.1.6 Part D: summary

Part D of the topic guide had one question that provided some very interesting data, which was, 'How did you feel about talking with me about [content]?' This question appeared to give the participant freedom to speak about what was covered in the interview, akin to active field notes.

Questions that worked well during the first phase of pilot interviews (n = 6) remained on the revised topic guide. I made some methodological modifications after the first phase of pilot interviews, where I made the questions more general. I was concerned that amending the questions mid-study would interrupt the comparability of data, but Amabile (2019) made a similar change in her qualitative study of attitudes of retirement. The author had underestimated the importance of identity maintenance in her initial interview protocol. This proved to be a rich and complex emergent theme, so identity questions were expanded half-way through data collection. I believe that there was no detriment to the continuity and comparability of interviews due to the slight amendment in questions.

3.2.1.7 Ethics and informed consent

A Research Ethics Application was approved for this study. Data collected throughout this study at all times respected the individual participant with regards to their dignity, respect, privacy, anonymity and confidentiality. As principal investigator (PI), I gained informed written consent from all participants. I provided participants with a 'Participant Information Sheet' (PIS). The PIS was provided prior to interview, and participants were given plenty of time to read the two-page document alone while I went to make them a cup of tea. Upon my return, I took the signed PIS and provided the participant with £10 payment. The topic guide for interviews was not seen by the participant; equally, it was not actively hidden from them.

It was Riach et al.'s (2016) reference to the interview 'set up' that resonated with my experience within this project. I had several participants who wanted to change the pre-agreed location upon arrival, which unsettled the initial meeting of the parties. For example, one participant wanted to be interviewed in a shared office space, well within hearing of at least six colleagues. I suggested they might be more comfortable in a private office, as I had previously indicated in our email correspondence. I was then challenged by the participant that I was requesting the private space for my own comfort, not theirs. Whether this was power or discomfort, instances such as this acted to create an uncomfortable start. At all times, however, I was mindful of the ethical considerations of the study.

3.3 Data analysis and 'writing up'

3.3.1 Transcription

I approached the transcription as a process of analysis, whereby the resulting transcription created an artefact within the broader book. There are few empirical accounts of transcribing; as such, I created my own method of coding and abbreviations. I have noticed that transcription rarely features in method sections of studies (whether papers, articles, books or book chapters), but I chose to include a section on the act of transcription within this book. For me, transcription is the first stage of analysis, and as such, I decided to conduct this myself rather than outsource the action to a third party, or to an AI-driven automated system. This resulted in my intimate knowledge of the data, as the transcription process required a four-times reading/listening of the data. I also transcribed my own post-interview field notes, which formed part of the data. I made a critical choice about transcription (Huff, 2009) that I was not apart from the data – that it was an embodied activity and interpretation whereby the nuances of the spoken word had to be accurately reflected in the transcript. The transcription activity was physically, as well as mentally, exhausting and became a deeply immersive experience.[1]

While a constructionist epistemology might suggest that no transcription is accurate (Huff, 2009), I believe that my transcripts reflect a true nature (not necessarily the true nature) of participant experiences. However, there were times during the transcription when I felt that the conversation was tangential, raising the question of whether to transcribe everything or whether it was sufficient to make an early call on what was irrelevant data (such as around our children's activities or a conversation around 'therapets' which happened to be in the office that day). Tangential sections remained as audio files and I entered a time stamp at start and end for these brief excluded sections. In keeping with the General Data Protection Regulation (GDPR) guidelines of the European Union (EU), I de-personalised and anonymised transcripts prior to analysis with the software package NVivo, replacing names with pseudonyms and redacting tell-tale place and profession information. The full, unredacted transcripts were held securely on the university server (within NVivo) and only viewed by myself and project colleagues.

3.3.2 *Data analysis: first stage*

Reflexivity is intrinsically processual (Alvesson et al., 2008): reflexivity is a process, not a thing. As a researcher, I was not only an active participant in the data collection, but also in the data analysis (Shaw & Langman, 2017), as it was I who identified and interpreted the themes. Data were analysed based on Braun and Clarke's (2006) thematic analysis. Data were coded to nodes, which became parent nodes once data were coded within them, creating a nesting effect of sub-themes. I coded as much of the data as was relevant to the research questions – I did not code 100% of the data, as some were tangential to the subject (for example, where rapport was being built or disruptions were made). However, the majority of data were coded within the developing hierarchy of codes.

Following Shaw and Langman's (2017) caution, while I maintained neutrality when possible, it was inevitable that my own perceptions, assumptions, bias, knowledge, understanding and research choices were imprinted on the data analysis process. These were likely myriad and too complex to identify or unravel; I adopted an impartial and open mind by allowing the data to speak through the iterative process of inductive analysis.

3.3.3 *Data analysis: second stage*

Analysis was conducted both within-person and between-person. Within-person analysis of individual stories around identity work in organisations allow the researcher to understand the 'complexities, contradictions and especially the struggles in their accounts' (Riach et al., 2016, p. 2071). Between-person analysis allowed for comparative analysis between individuals by a myriad of factors including age, lifestyle, domestic factors, health and occupational status. Starting as inductive, the analysis became 'fine grained' through iteration.

At this point, I closely followed Corley and Gioia's (2004) method of data structure, identifying first order themes using participant voice as the source of data. Once data were coded to these first-order codes, I then conducted thematic analysis to create a series of second-order themes, which then were developed over time in an iterative process into 'aggregate dimensions'.

I also conducted an element of deductive analysis in this book on data that were provided in response to my direct question: 'What does the term "successful ageing" mean to you?' This question was initially informed by the literature review. As I mentioned earlier in this book, I have an element of scepticism about how this term is accepted by participants, and I was curious about how this might have been interpreted. I believed that it was important to understand how the people I was researching felt about a key term we academics use about those very people. The concept of successful ageing and indeed participant responses to the concept remains an important theme and catalyst for data around the ageing body.

3.3.3.1 *Analysing gender and 'class'*

Broader class structures have explanatory power in understanding the construction of the self (Savage, 2015), and this aspect of structural inequality should not be overlooked in a book on gendered ageing at work. Gendered economic inequalities felt by workers in mid- to later life are a result of a complex web of interweaving factors (Price et al., 2016; Brown & Vickerstaff, 2011). For example, gender inequalities in flexible working forms such as self-employment are characterised by higher levels of choice, autonomy and control for men, and less so for women, especially women with lower educational attainment and socio-economic backgrounds (Loretto & Vickerstaff, 2015). Further, Krekula (2009) suggested that jobs are not only coded by gender and age, but are also socially coded. Similarly, caring roles are found to be not only gendered, but also age-typed (Loretto & White, 2006), bringing into focus the multiplicity of inequality felt across the life course, which highlights developmental trajectories affecting labour force participation of women around three core areas: cumulative (dis)advantage, gender norms and domestic constraints (Damaske & Frech, 2016; Damaske, 2011).

While I could have addressed class through the middle classes, which 'rest precariously between privilege and vulnerability' (Skeggs, 2004), class is not a focus in this book due to the narrow class categories of participants. Further, while participants in this book are generally 'middle-class', there is significant variability in occupational status, income and educational attainment, i.e. the generally accepted measures of class (Livingstone & Scholtz,

2016). However, I do report on aspects of cumulative (dis)advantage over the gendered life course (Riach et al., 2015). Class can be an embarrassing and unsettling topic (Sayer, 2005), more so than gender in contemporary identity narratives (Gray & Kish-Gephart, 2013), suggesting a socially agreed permission to acknowledge gender in a way that class is not openly discussed. Even here there is a reluctance to foreground or discuss class due to insufficient class differences to perform what some organisational scholars personally informed me should consider an essential comparison between blue and white-collar workers. Instead, the book draws distinction through occupational differences due to a focus on individual work contexts.

3.4 Reflexivity of researching workers in mid- to later life

I was inspired by Alvesson et al.'s (2008) work, which contrary to a positivistic model seeks to construct alternative understandings of concepts that have been marginalised. This resonated with me in that it clearly delineated between positivism and constructionism, but also addressed a key feature of the participants that I was getting to know through my data collection, i.e. the potentially marginalised worker. I adopted Alvesson et al.'s (2008) advocacy of the merits of reflexive research, but heeded their warning as to whether organisational research sufficiently engages in reflexivity: 'for us, reflexivity is not primarily an end in itself, but a means to improve research in some way' (Alvesson et al., 2008). This book, therefore, is an attempt to be 'sufficiently reflexive' by mapping my research experience on to the development of this research project.

Bourdieu described the need for the researcher to engage in 'participant objectivation' (Bourdieu, 1977) in order to situate themselves within the social space, i.e. the interview space. Kerr and Robinson (2011) cited Wacquant's (2008) work on the 'epistemological privilege' of the native by stating the awareness that they, as authors, were excluded from the field of their investigation – in their case, the elite banking field – and as such must make their reportage from an external viewpoint. Gioia et al. (2012) also addressed this issue of 'going native' or being too close to the participant view, which is a risk of conducting qualitative research and can be mitigated by adopting a 'devil's advocate' role to critique interviewer assumptions. In applying this concept to my own relational position with my interview participants, I engaged in identity work as a reflexive researcher, understanding myself as half-in/half-out, or occupying that liminal space between the entry point of middle-aged, but not yet an 'older worker'.

Reflexivity within the interview space is also enabled through an element of reciprocity, following Alvesson and Skoldberg (2000):

> There is no one-way street between the researcher and the object of study; rather, the two affect each other mutually and continually in the course of the research process. A positivistic conception of research,

according to which the object is uninfluenced by the researcher and the researcher is unaffected by the object, is thus untenable.

Towards the end of the interviews, I actively engaged with Bourdieu's (1984) 'reflexivity in practice', or 'doing reflexivity'. This was a more conscious way of approaching reflexivity within the interview and subsequent analysis process. Johnson and Duberley (2003, p. 1289) posited that 'epistemic reflexivity must relate to how a researcher's own social location affects the forms and outcomes of research as well as entailing acceptance of the conviction that there will always be more than one valid account of any research'. Further, Ford and Harding (2011) suggested that a 'reflexive undoing' should contrast with an organisational undoing to develop our understanding of how individuals experience conformity as 'viable social subjects' within their organisational field. As such, I reflected on how my own social position within different fields affected on my own researcher habitus (Bourdieu, 1984).

For example, I concur with Julia Twigg (2012) who, when writing about her work on attire and the older woman, said, 'I too have puzzled over what to wear as I get older and this has fed into my work . . . . It is also significant to write as a woman'. I was able to connect with my female participants in a particular way as I am female, there was a sense that sensitive, personal matters were more easily discussed due to our within-gender dynamic.

Reflexive research and developing my researcher habitus will continue – perhaps this work in progress will be a constant companion throughout my academic career without a logical completion or end date. In summary, I believe that my age and gender was a benefit in researching gendered bodily ageing, specifically relating to same-sex participants. Learning about reflexive research must come from doing reflexive research by maintaining a reflexive attitude to learning about how to meet, interview and interact with participants. It is important to carefully balance this self-awareness with de-emphasising the self. It is, after all, the participants' story, not mine, however integral my role as reflexive researcher is to the research process.

3.5 Participant findings relating to method

Data revealed that some participants voluntarily gave reasons for what motivated their participation in this study. I present these findings here rather than in the main result chapters of this book, treating them as methodological findings around participation. These findings reflected two main themes. First, participants explicitly recognised the importance and value of research and wanted to contribute for that reason. Second, some participants were looking for a platform from which to express their experiences of a specific aspect of their experiences at work. Interestingly, although a cash payment of £10 was offered and accepted by most participants, this was clearly not the motive for participation.

While most participants showed an interest in the subject of enquiry (the ageing body) and how it was being explored (appearance), some participants explicitly discussed their appreciation of the value of the research and an interest in the research output. Monica, for example, was a research nurse and was familiar with the process of research and its importance. She indicated this to be her reason for volunteering to participate in the interview and empathised with how difficult it can be to find participants for studies. Participants who were results driven were specifically looking for information on ageing at work due to the paucity of available information relevant to them.

> . . . when I heard you were doing this I said yes, I want to get involved 'cause I just feel [menopause] is so debilitating . . .
>
> (Vera, 56, event manager)

> . . . although I'm mildly horrified to know that I'm regarded as the older workforce, I am interested in that ageing process and what that looks like.
>
> (Julia, 50, teacher)

It was clear that some participants had their own agenda prior to interview. This speaks to Riach et al.'s (2016) experience of 'reflexive undoing', whereby participants started by discussing their own achievements at the start of the interview. Data here extend this finding that participants set up a platform through self-deprecating talk. Isla, for example, felt the frustration at the lack of agency at being able to make meaningful change at work with regard to procedural changes that would support her desire to work more flexible hours:

> I'm just not senior enough to do anything about them [good ideas]; that's the problem.
>
> (Isla, 58, project manager)

Kara's following comment summarised a common sentiment from participants when discussing retirement age. The emotions were of anger and frustration at not being able to retire at an age previously planned prior to the increase of the state pension age (SPA). Her narrative throughout the interview was focused on this point from the very beginning and while she offered much in terms of long monologues in response to the questions asked, her narrative continually returned to her feelings of injustice of having to work longer.

> I've been working a long time and had expectation of retiring at 60 and I was close enough within – I can't remember what the year was, but I'm a '56 birthday, it must have been something like 52 or 53, that was the cut off, I was just too close to it . . . all my friends are retired because they can be, because they are still married and therefore for whatever reason their incomes allow it, so they are coffee-ing or walking or exercising, not having to get up . . .
>
> (Kara, 62, secretary)

Laura spoke of the difficulty of continuing a workload that she had carried throughout her career as teacher. Due to bodily ageing processes, specifically the effects of menopause symptoms, she was 'unable to maintain' previous levels of activity and workload. Like Kara, she felt angry and let down by structural factors (SPA increase, inflexibility of her employer to accommodate her menopause symptoms) and by her ageing body. Her interview was dominated by a discourse of anger, much of what she said in the interview she had 'never said out loud before' so her narrative felt raw and emotional. In our post-interview discussion, Laura confided that she had nobody to talk to at work about her experiences and feelings of ageing and took this as an opportunity to make her voice heard:

> It's a very busy day. It's an interesting thing, because it's made very clear, once you pass the interview stage to accepting a job that you have to commit to . . . what they call the whole life of the school . . . . So that is another bone of contention . . . because for older people it simply becomes more and more and more difficult to do [additional] activities and there is no reference at all to people in different stages in their careers as to who should do what as they age.
>
> (Laura, 50, teacher)

3.6 Literature review as method

The literature review is featured in this method chapter for two reasons: first, due to its integral role within the iterative process of analysis; and second, due to its role in creating the research design. Crafting the literature view was akin to completing a jigsaw puzzle. I could see every individual piece clearly, but how they fit together seemed bewildering at first. The task would be impossible without the picture on the front of the box, so I created a book contents page to act as a guide. While this was forever changing, it was integral to have a 'map-for-now' in order to make sense of the broad range of literature that I had accumulated over the first two years of writing this book. It came to a point that I had so many papers filed in my online research folder, many printed waiting to be included, that I had read some of these, made notes in others, briefly summarised others. In June 2019, I called a halt to reading and needed to make sense of what I had. I emptied out the 'jigsaw puzzle box' onto my desk. It was a mountain of small pieces that all looked like blue sky. Slowly but surely, I could discern different shades of blue, different shades of green for the forest and slightly different textures of brown for the mountain. With my seemingly simple contents outline, I started putting it all together – borders first, then painstakingly little sections of pieces started to fit together. It took three months to create the 'jigsaw puzzle' from the 'box', and by the end of the summer I had a coherent set up for a research question that addressed a gap in the literature as well as joining a broader social and organisational conversation. This was also informed by the data that I had started to analyse at that point, thus creating the iterative loop between primary data and secondary research.

It was the aim of this chapter to provide the reader with a sense of evolution of how this book was developed from a methodological perspective. This chapter also presented the rationale for adopting a social constructionist epistemology and a subjective ontology that sought ways to explore and address the research objective and questions. I have also subsequently drawn upon the principles laid out in Riach et al. (2016), who wrote about a 'reflexive undoing' through qualitative research. I considered how their approach to the interview as a performative act related to how I conducted interviews, whereby the researcher and method should be part of the 'constitution of the subject'. I hope this detailed account of my methodological approach to this study is of practical use to academics and practitioners wishing to conduct their own research study.

Note

1 Since I conducted the transcription to which I refer here, artificial intelligence (AI) has improved significantly. I have recently used AI to transcribe some interview data, and the act of reviewing these outputs did bring me close to the data, so perhaps this is a middle ground.

4 Identity work of the ageing body at work

Shielding, capitalising and negative self-affirmation

Individual differences played a role in how identity work was conducted to maintain not only participation, but a valuable contribution to labour force. Participants appeared to navigate liminality by striving to maintain a status quo of perceived performance at work, which was not possible for all participants due to perceptions of self and others around natural bodily ageing. Specifically, data revealed that individual trait confidence and authenticity of identity were entwined with participants' emotional responses to their ageing bodies at work (Goretzki & Messner, 2019; Caza et al., 2018; Winkler, 2018). Previous work has highlighted that confidence, authenticity and emotional identity narratives are potentially connected (Winkler, 2018; Caza et al., 2018). This study shows that identity work was motivated by – and arguably was contingent upon – confidence and authenticity, and was presented through an emotive identity discourse around the importance of the appearance of bodily ageing within the individuals' work context.

Building on previous studies on meta-perceptions (Meister et al., 2014), data showed a differential influence in how participants were vulnerable to or were able to shield against internalised ageism. Internalised ageism has been previously reported as experienced through the body (Hurd Clarke & Korotchenko, 2016; Hurd Clarke & Griffin, 2008) and conducted through a social construction of what it means to be 'older' (Phelan, 2018). The contextual view of experiencing the ageing body in this book provides a nuanced insight into the how, why and from whom do women in mid- to later life draw on perceptions of self and others to protect against or become vulnerable to internalised ageism at work.

Emotions – specifically, an emotional response to the gendered ageing body – could influence how worker identity was (re)produced and how identity work was conducted. Findings suggest that there was no dominant direction in how emotions trigger or lead to identity work (Winkler, 2018), but rather that the relationship was somewhat chaotic, reflective of research on identity construction and negotiation at work as 'chaotic, sometimes contradictory collections' of self (Alvesson et al., 2008; Jones & Clifton, 2018). Expanding on current thinking on emotions and identity work, this chapter provides evidence that identity work was conducted through an emotive

DOI: 10.4324/9781003439257-4

dialogue, fuelled by external sources of expectations around gendered ageing and ageism at work.

Confidence, or lack thereof, was explicitly referred to in participant discourse. Participants drew on the term directly, or the concept indirectly, to express their experiences of gendered bodily ageing at work. At no point were participants asked to comment on confidence directly in the interviews. Those who described confidence indirectly or conceptually rather than directly did so through a discourse of high self-esteem, ease, assurance and comfort in their ageing bodies at work. Conversely, confidence was also discussed as a declining resource, conducted through a discourse of bodily dissociation, 'what's wrong with me?' or reduction of self, 'shrink' or 'hiding'.

A dialogue around confidence was an emotional discourse; confidence was seemingly inseparable from emotions, both positive and negative, in how participants understood their ageing bodies. Confidence and emotions are intertwined in how emotional experiences can act as a trigger of identity work caused by identity threats (Winkler, 2018), but also by identity opportunities. These identity threats and opportunities emerged from the inter-relationship between a potentially threatened sense of confidence and an assessment of an authentic work identity through an emotionally charged discourse of bodily ageing at work. These aspects of confidence, authenticity and emotion were contingent upon perceptions of self and others around the contextual importance of bodily ageing at work.

This chapter reports on three sub-themes of how identity work was conducted through navigating the gendered ageing body at work. The liminar differentially engaged in identity work whereby confidence and authenticity worked to regulate an emotional discourse around being perceived as looking older at work. First, shielding from internalised ageism was enabled by relevant and valued experiences and an expression of positive emotions, high confidence and high unconditional authenticity. Second, capitalising on an ageing aesthetic was reported by women, as an ageing aesthetic has been reported more frequently as favouring the male body at work (Foweraker & Cutcher, 2019; Calasanti & King, 2018; Hurd Clarke, 2018). Third, negative self-affirmation was conducted by women, which was overwhelmingly presented in relation to experiencing and managing menopause symptoms at work.[1] As discussed in the literature review, identity work is considered highly agentic and yet empirical studies have placed insufficient importance on the role of individualised work context and the structural constraints or opportunities that arise (Brown, 2015).

Findings suggest that identity work was highly gendered and structural factors provided an institutionalised context of relational influence of out-group others. This chapter explores emotions through a discursive focus, or the words used to describe emotional responses to identity tensions and threats (Beech, 2011), allowing a more nuanced understanding of how identity work is motivated by emotional responses to identity transitions in how women in mid- to later life work.

4.1 Shielding from internalised ageism

A minority of female (six of 21) participants discussed an increase in confidence that they associated with age and associated experience: 'been around the block a bit' (Georgina, 55). A sense of confidence was communicated by participants who worked in positions of seniority and described their work identity through a positive discourse of optimism, excitement and enthusiasm. Participants with a strong sense of their authentic self at work engaged in dialogic identity work, which was a self-affirming, positive portrayal of their work identity, their work performance and a sense of security in their position within the world of work. Positive identity talk portrayed these participants as liminars, of being older-not-old and yet there was a sense of ease for some workers and evidence of an identity opportunity for others. In this scenario, liminality was viewed with a positive emotional response as a socially legitimate narrative with a known outcome (Turner, 1969).

Participants who engaged in an emotionally confident discourse did so through an awareness of the appearance of their bodily ageing. Participants in this category engaged in neutral or negative personal descriptors, or negative body talk. However, their trait confidence and high work identity authenticity within the world of work acted as a form of 'shield' against negative identity talk of self or worker identity. This shield was extended against perception of self and others, suggesting a relatively short journey along a highly ritualised path of liminality. This narrative of confidence at work, despite neutral or negative dialogic identity work centred around the body, was conducted by participants who worked in senior positions and by their own admission had few menopause symptoms at work.

Participants displaying dialogic identity work through trait confidence acknowledged their increasing age and changing bodies due to ageing, and yet their heightened security in their sense of self at work was associated with an increased security in their work identity. This was displayed by acceptance of self and perceived acceptance by meaningful others at work, such as younger colleagues.

Women in this category presented a complex relationship between confidence and their authentic work identity. A nuanced distinction to this was that despite positive dialogic identity work, there remained an awareness that as an older worker, there was a perceived requirement to work harder. While the quote from Georgina, a 55-year-old director, is used to exemplify this point, it should be stated that she did not feel as if being a woman negatively affected her work identity or work opportunities; her concern over discrimination was around her age only, not her gender. Paradoxically, age and experience increased her confidence at work and yet her age was the factor to which she attributed having to work harder and was exposed to workplace discrimination:

> I think [age] is a positive dimension to my working life, perhaps that's something that comes from within. I definitely feel much more

> self-confident, I feel that I've got a lot of experience . . . you become the senior people in the world of work, you're not intimidated in the way you used to be . . . [but] as you get older you have to put more effort in . . . I worked all the way through having three children . . . very challenging in terms of sexist attitudes and logistics . . . I've reached a stage in my life where my kids are independent and I want to work more . . . it's easier for me to work.

The inter-relationship between confidence and the authentic self was also affected by the extent to which opinions or perceptions of meaningful others at work were internalised as ageism by the individual. Further, a comparison with one's younger self also contributed to how participant discourse of confidence contributed to the stability of their work identity. Participants reporting high confidence – as with the preceding examples – acknowledged objective bodily ageing as change or even decline, and yet their work identity was robust against these bodily changes. Confidence was also acknowledged to compensate for the physical appearance of an ageing body in relation to a younger self.

> Dried elbows, cellulite and saggy knees . . . I think where have my pretty little knees gone? Again, in my inflated sense of confidence, I still look and think oh it does work [laughs].
>
> (Rachel, 50, lawyer)

> I decided at 50 that I was just going to stop dyeing it and go grey, and that was a confidence, self-esteem thing, and I feel better for it.
>
> (Monica, 53, nursery nurse)

Confidence appeared to be embraced by older workers to shield them against ageing assumptions and stereotypes. The appearance of their ageing bodies at work, however, appeared to be contingent upon individual perception within their role and performance with the organisation:

> I think confidence shields you from ageism . . . people can persuade themselves that they are hard done by because they are female . . . because they are older, but actually are they performing to the best of their ability . . . at a level where they are competing properly?
>
> (Rachel, 50, lawyer).

4.2 Capitalising on an ageing aesthetic: a precarious state

For some participants, becoming older at work saw engagement in largely experimental identity work to reposition work identity with the liminal position of older-not-old. The precarity of the ability to capitalise on the appearance of bodily ageing was contingent upon perceptions of and connections with out-group others. For these women, the ageing body was explicitly situated to represent wisdom and experience to younger out-group members (both male and female). There was a submission to the ageing body – again engaging in neutral or negative identity work about the ageing body. However, confidence in work ability and in themselves – suggesting an enduring trait confidence – enabled identity work of reinvention or repositioning in relation to a younger audience. While the relative identity of older-and-wiser was embraced as an accepted work identity, the emotional acceptance of this was contingent upon seemingly transient feelings of vulnerability and confidence associated with an ageing body. Confidence was maintained through and almost anchored to an authentic presentation of the body; however, for some participants, their body-related confidence was rooted in the appearance of their younger bodies. Arguably, confidence was complexly enmeshed with emotional responses to an ageing body, but these experiences appear to be contextualised based on perceptions of mainly out-group others at work.

While being and looking older at work was associated by many participants as a positive aspect of their visibly ageing bodies at work, it was for some a contingent identity based on emotional response. The formation of new work identities was conducted through a negotiation of one's authentic self. An acceptance of the ageing body, albeit through neutral and sometimes negative discourse, foregrounded the appearance of ageing in a reconstructed worker identity. The most common example of this was for the participant to position themselves as different from younger colleagues, foregrounding tenure or the value of experience, which was communicated through the appearance of ageing, or looking older. A maternal body was performed and presented through identity work associated with positive emotions of trust, ease and happiness.

> . . . it's nice to think that you are trusted
>
> (Penny)

> I feel like I'm their mum . . . I love that.
>
> (Rachel)

> there is something about the role you fulfil . . . the role of good mother.
>
> (Deborah)

The female body, however, gave cause for interrupted confidence, which jeopardised this identity work of maternalism. For example, Isla, a 58-year-old project manager, demonstrated a within-person conflict whereby her acceptance of her work identity as her team's 'wise owl' was contingent upon the variability of her level of emotional confidence, which she attributed in part to her menopause symptoms.

> . . . you're the wise owl . . . actually I'm not as old as you think I am, you know. You like it, but you don't like it . . . if you're feeling vulnerable you take it as a personal thing, if you're feeling confident, you just go oh cool.

Similarly, acceptance of the appearance of natural bodily ageing, 'sagging' and 'wrinkles' is a challenge to confidence. For example, Penny, a 51-year-old teacher, attributed her unofficial pastoral role towards younger colleagues to her ageing appearance, which conveyed her life experience. Unlike the previously mentioned participants, this role was not sought and was not particularly welcomed by Penny; however, she was aware of the changing dynamic between herself and her younger colleagues. She was dialogically experimenting with a maternal identity, not yet accepting or rejecting this role chosen by out-group others:

> [Weight] appears in places that you had never put on weight before and that can be hard for people's confidence . . . [you] feel the ageing process, the sagging and nothing looks right, that's just part of parcel of getting old isn't it? . . . I get everyone's problems . . . because I look old and people think I've been through a lot more, I've got quite a lot more wrinkles that they have, oh she's had these traumas so she might know the answer . . . [she] won't be so frivolous.

Identity work was conducted to reposition work identity to gain relevance or value within the work context, which extended to changing how participants work not only to capitalise on an ageing aesthetic but to accommodate actual bodily changes in performance. This was exemplified by Deborah, 53, who changed how she worked due to the physical toll of work on her ageing body. Her new job was, in part, selected in response to perceptions of others around her ageing body. She also displayed a within-person contradiction of embracing an older worker aesthetic as a new work identity, while dissociating with aspects of this category, i.e. the post-menopausal body.

> I gave up the [manual job] as it was too physically strenuous and I thought what would I like to do instead and I chose counselling because I thought it would be the one thing that would accommodate the fact that I was an older woman . . . my sense was that women [in mid- to later life] are actually celebrated in a way that they are often not celebrated in other areas of work . . . . So, I am now post-menopausal, which I don't like, I don't like that label . . . . No, makes me feel old.
>
> (Deborah, 53, counsellor)

4.3 Negative self-affirmation

Data revealed that a number of women spoke about their ageing body through a discourse of negative emotions including fear, disgust, shame and surprise. This dialogic interaction with their changing, ageing bodies had an adverse impact on their work identity and attitudes towards how they could or wanted to work in future. This narrative of negative self-affirmation was often conducted by drawing on available discourses of older (Ybema et al., 2009), specifically through a comparison with participants' younger selves and with younger colleagues. Reduced confidence, discussed through negative identity work, was prevalent. Women who engaged in negative self-affirmation referred to self-confidence as that which was either in decline or was under threat. This derogation of a personal trait of individual difference – i.e. confidence, self-assurance, self-efficacy – was presented as a negative emotional experience for these workers, all of whom were female. The loss of confidence appeared to directly affect how women engaged in dialogue with and about themselves and their ageing bodies within the world of work. Further, participant discourse of low confidence-related negative identity work was self-affirming through gendered agency: 'I did it to myself'.

What was clear from the data was that women who experienced a sense that their appearance of bodily ageing was in decline – whether objectively true or not, and whether perceptions of others were real or not – also experienced reduced confidence at work. Gendered agency in the liminal identity work that women used to position themselves in this sense of subordination to out-group others at work, but also to models of their younger selves, appeared to be associated with a lack of control over and confidence in their ageing bodies. This emotional response to reduced confidence due to a decline in physical appearance was exemplified by Adele and Catherine, both speaking in reference to their younger selves.

> I was more confident, I think being blonde and you know, young and attractive helped my confidence . . . . I've had a bit of a rude shock to my system in the last year going from feeling quite good for my age to feeling like a tremendous old bag.
>
> (Adele, 50, doctor)

> I was skinny, I [wore] a really nice suit . . . my hair used to be much redder than it is now, it's faded as I've gotten older . . . my appearance had something to do with my confidence . . .
>
> (Catherine, 51, counsellor)

The disturbance of life-long trait of confidence appeared to lead to a dissociation with work identity. This separation of self from confident worker to unconfident worker created a sense of liminality due to the uncertainty and transitional nature of the decline in confidence. While confidence was in reduction – or in some cases was viewed as 'gone' – the mechanisms behind the change were gendered ageing/ageism, including menopause as well perceived physical decline. This decline in confidence resulted in being absent from work and perceptions of having to demonstrate continued or even improved performance:

> . . . complete lack of confidence, confidence gone.
>
> (Vera, 56, events manager – speaking in relation to the impact of menopause symptoms at work)

> I think you are being perceived in a different way, by younger staff . . . as if they think you're not going to manage . . . maybe it's our confidence diminishing.
>
> (Penny, 51, teacher)

As discussed, perceptions of younger colleagues appeared to be a key motivator in determining how participants spoke about their ageing bodies. In direct response to a personal comparison with younger colleagues in terms of age and physical attributes of different-aged bodies, self and worker identity was challenged. Emotional responses of shame, self-doubt and insecurity led to reduced confidence; this lowered confidence, resulted in 'hiding' evidence of natural biological changes of an ageing female body that, for some, was once a source of personal pride. Menopause was a source of gendered ageing, the emotional and physical symptoms of which appeared to directly impact confidence at work, which in turn appeared to influence labour force participation decisions. Internalised ageism led to a negative discourse or identity talk around the ageing body as a result of menopause itself, but also as a result of perceptions of others, i.e. how participants reacted based on how they thought younger colleagues were perceiving them. This negative self-affirmation was exemplified by Deborah as she discussed perceptions of her ageing and menopausal body at work:

> . . . something about being surrounded by young skinnies [made] me shrink a bit (long pause). . . . I'm hiding the weight gain . . . it's post-menopausal . . . I am not the young hourglass I used to be [long pause] and yet I want to be heard . . . my husband has a bit of a tum and he's accepted.
>
> (Deborah, 53, counsellor)

While menopause was associated with a discourse of vulnerability and a threatened identity through a decline in confidence, agentic identity work to consciously improve appearance at work resulted in a sense of reclaiming confidence; identity work transferred to a different area of appearance, from the naked unadorned body to the covering of the body. However, changes to conform to organisational standards also worked to undermine a sense of authenticity. This concept was illustrated by Tania, a 50-year-old academic, who admitted to a reduction in confidence that was entwined with a discourse of vulnerability around the impact of menopause symptoms and increased workload on her perceived and actual abilities at work. She referred to a reclaiming of confidence through a conscious change in physical appearance in terms of her choice of work attire. Despite her confidence being reduced by physical changes to her ageing body, she was able to experience an increase in confidence through presentation of her body in line with the expectations of her male colleagues, although this confidence appeared situational and precarious.

> . . . I dressed smarter and that gave me more confidence . . . to change my appearance and look more professional at work . . . with male peers . . . .

Findings highlight how participants internalise gendered ageism through age-related mechanisms such as menopause and the perceived need to confirm to gendered ageist expectations of out-group others.

4.4 Chapter discussion

Identity is said to bridge the gap between the individual self and society or social structures whereby identity is constructed through discourse; discursive articulation of identity is seen as an ongoing iteration between what is projected and what is perceived (Ybema et al., 2009). This was borne out by participants who engaged in identity work around their ageing bodies largely in relation to how they believed that they were perceived by self and others at work. This chapter demonstrates how, through shielding from internalised ageism, capitalising on an ageing aesthetic and engaging in negative self-affirmation of bodily ageing, participants differentially made sense of, performed and displayed their ageing bodies through a liminal state, engaging in (un)emotional identity work (Table 4.1).

Within the broader exploration of how women in mid- to later life experience bodily ageing at work, this chapter answered how individual differences lead to dialogic practices around bodily ageing. Participants spoke of their emotions in relation to the perceived and actual appearance of their ageing bodies in a number of ways. Emotions such as anger were expressed regarding the extension of the state pension age (SPA) and having to engage the ageing body to work for longer. Anxiety (Ibarra & Petriglieri, 2007), fear and insecurity were expressed to describe natural biological changes of the gendered ageing body. Further, participants displayed aspects of ageing anxiety, which supports previous findings that ageing anxiety not only affects one's own perceptions of ageing (Carter, 2016), but that those who experienced ageing anxiety themselves were more likely to stereotype based on age or avoid those of a similar age (Shaw & Langman, 2017). Specifically, this chapter showed how this appearance-based ageing anxiety led into internalised ageism. However, participants also described feelings of optimism and ease at experiencing an authentic connection with their ageing bodies at work. Previous research suggests that emotions will be either positively or negatively expressed, depending on whether identity work is presented as an opportunity or threat (Winkler, 2018); however, evidence here suggests that it is not quite so binary.

Successful identity work was contingent upon freedom and confidence to feel an authenticity of self. Shielding was conducted by participants who experienced positive emotions, resulting in high emotional confidence towards understanding their ageing bodies at work. These participants enjoyed a strong sense of worker identity and spoke of an unconditional acceptance of their bodies experiencing high personal authenticity of identity. While identity work around the body was neutral or even negative, this was generally reconciled through identity work of not placing an emphasis on the ageing body. Participants engaged in a dialogic construction that was 'inside-out initiation'; however, there was little sense of experimentation, as with the Beech (2011) model, in that a consistency and authenticity of worker identity seemingly did not require it.

In terms of liminality, there was evidence of a dissociation between younger and older self; however, this was reconciled through an emotionally

Table 4.1 Chapter 4 findings – Study 1

Dialogic identity work	*Trait confidence*	*Authenticity of work identity*	*Emotional response to ageing*	*Dialogic descriptors*	*Liminality*	*Themes*
Shielding	High	High: unconditional acceptance	Optimism, excitement, enthusiasm	Neutral/ negative	Reconciled	Confidence shields against internalised ageism
Capitalising	Contingent on emotional state	Fluctuating: in negotiation	Trust, acceptance, submission, apprehension	Neutral/ negative	Recognised	Capitalising on an ageing aesthetic: eldership
Negative self-affirmation	Low, in decline, disrupted	Low: threatened	Sadness, disgust, anger, fear, surprise	Negative	Unreconciled, unreconcilable	Invisibility, self-deprecation

confident discourse. Liminality reflected Turner's (1969) classic conceptualisation whereby workers followed a socially legitimate narrative of the ageing body. Participant experiences were highly institutionalised and suggested that the liminar followed an already established path through ageing (Ibarra & Obodaru, 2016). Interestingly, these participants were women who not only worked in male sex-type roles but by their own admission experienced very little bodily change from the ageing process, specifically referring to menopause. All were highly confident individuals over their life course without disruption from experiences or interpretations of their ageing bodies. As Winkler (2018) posited, positive emotions were presented as identity work without threat to their work identity.

Capitalising on the ageing aesthetic was conducted by participants who experienced emotions in relation to ageing including trust, acceptance of self, submission to the ageing process, anticipation of being an 'older worker' and what that meant to them, as well as apprehension of the physical changes associated with ageing. As with shielding, data showed that emotions triggered liminal identity work and identity work was an emotional process (Winkler, 2018). The fluidity of emotional confidence was experienced by women, for whom trait confidence was reported as stable across the life course, but was now contingent upon their emotional and arguably hormonal state in response to menopause symptoms. Worker authenticity of identity was in a state of flux and negotiation of self was conducted through experimental liminal identity practices (Beech, 2011), such as finding a new role identity at work based on the appearance of their ageing bodies as older. Beech (2011) positioned experimental liminal practices with an inside-out dialogic construction, but findings here suggest that experimental identity work was conducted through perceptions of others, seeking their approval in some ways for assurance of the reposition of the older worker as the mature figure of experience and wisdom. This most commonly manifested as a maternal or paternal identity in relation to younger colleagues.

Emotions can be used to 'construct and maintain preferred versions of self', (re)producing discourses which constitute identity positions (Kuhn, 2009; Ahuja et al., 2019). Data here suggested that the transitional or liminal aesthetic of ageing presented an opportunity for a reconstruction of worker identity but this was limited to an identity associated with looking older. As such, it was not presented as a preferred version of self, but an available, socially acceptable and opportunistic reconstruction of worker identity. Emotions are crucial to how individuals define themselves (Fineman, 2003), expanded here as emotions being crucial in how workers reinvent and reposition work identity through identity work. Identity work processes of balancing work or role identities has been reported to result in negative emotions of vulnerability and stress (Beech et al., 2012); however, data suggest here that a relatively forced reinvention due to the obligatory nature of liminality (Turner, 1969) for some participants was actually a positive experience with positive work outcomes, albeit one of necessity and reduced options.

Liminality was resolved by workers in this group through reinvention; repositioning of work identity, which was generally conducted through identity work based on perceptions; and/or reflections of others. Mapping against liminal identity work theory (Beech, 2011), participants engaged in liminal practices almost simultaneously – recognition of the ageing body, engaging in reflections and self-questioning in a changeful situation, while also experimenting with new role identities where the older body would be 'not only accepted but celebrated'. This simultaneous liminal practice culminated in resolution – or at least an acceptance – that the liminal state worked for them, that the older body could be viewed as a positive attribute in their world of work. Experiences were individual and highly contextual and reliant on acceptance of influential out-group members, suggesting that this model of total liminal practice was effortful and possibly precarious (Beech, 2008; Sveningsson & Alvesson, 2003). These findings extend existing theory of liminal identity work through the essential component of perceptions of others – specifically, out-group others, and within that category, 'younger' others included their younger selves.

The potentially chaotic nature of emotional engagement with the gendered ageing body by almost all participants suggested that the relationship between emotions and identity work is not as simple as positive and negative. Participants described menopause as rendering the ageing female body unpredictable, supporting previous work which referred to the older female body as 'out of place' at work and causing a lack of control over emotions (Acker, 1990; Jack et al., 2014; Grandey et al., 2020).

This chapter provides support for previous findings that identity talk is a strategy of tactical self-deprecation through conflicting organisational discourses (Down & Reveley, 2009), where self-alienation was a mechanism to reconcile a negotiation between putative 'real selves' (Costas & Fleming, 2009), and to preserve the integrity of self through separation of self and other (Clarke et al., 2009), and that identity work itself was used as a coping mechanism (Ahuja et al., 2019). Further, findings highlight that identity work was predicated and contingent upon uninterrupted confidence in the body at work and emotional responses to the appearance of bodily ageing, and how perceptions of others were agentically internalised or deflected. Contextualised experiences of the ageing body at work based on gender, job type, seniority at work and age of colleagues all contributed to how participants – through the influence of their emotions – were able to navigate the transitional nature of 'becoming' older at work.

Note

1 Menopause-specific findings from this study have been reported in academic journals articles Steffan (2021) and Steffan and Potočnik (2023); as such, these findings are not repeated here.

5 Successful ageing as value

Healthy and economic ageing

The aim of this chapter is to tease apart 'age' and 'ageing', which are often used interchangeably in the 'older worker' literature (Twigg, 2012; Taylor et al., 2016; Calasanti & King, 2018). Findings provide a response to a recent challenge to the adoption of chronological age and a call for rejection of chronological age from both quantitative researchers (Kotter-Grühn et al., 2016) and qualitative researchers (Krekula, 2007; Tulle & Krekula, 2013). Further, findings highlight the problematic nature of the unchallenged acceptance of the subjective, value-laden and ubiquitous label of 'successful' in describing the heterogenous nature of ageing at work (Carpentieri et al., 2016; Zacher, 2015; Abraham & Hansson, 1995). The following analysis provides insight into how workers over 50 interact with the term 'successful ageing' at work, reporting on who reproduces the concept of ideal worker as one who is successfully ageing (Rowe & Kahn, 1997, 2015) and how these concepts lead to working differently in later life, including early exit from the labour force. Bodily ageing was measured against chronological age: the majority of participants rejected subjectively looking and feeling older despite an understanding of their age and their objectively ageing body. The following analysis reports on this distinction of what successful ageing meant to workers over 50 years of age and who defines what successful ageing at work looks like.

An analysis of the data showed that all participants engaged with and actively discussed what successful ageing meant to them in the world of work. Data revealed that the majority of participants demonstrated an understanding and acknowledgement – even an acceptance, reluctant or willing – of chronological age, objective bodily ageing and being 'older' at work; however, participants overwhelmingly did not want to appear older. Participant reaction was overwhelmingly: 'be older, but don't look it'.

This within-person contradiction revealed two main themes of how the appearance of bodily ageing was managed by participants. First, the appearance of health was conducted as identity work to reduce the appearance of looking older. Participant focus was firmly on not only looking younger, but also feeling younger: healthy ageing. The exception to this was (un)healthy ageing through menopause symptoms, which was the only exclusively female

DOI: 10.4324/9781003439257-5

health-related theme to how workers in mid- to later life in this study discussed the concept of successful ageing as healthy ageing.

Second, identity work was engaged to promote the concept of the productive worker: economic ageing was discursive identity work conducted by participants. Here, findings show a distinction between the younger participants, i.e. younger than 60 years of age, and the older participants, more than 60 years of age. Younger workers in mid- to later life appeared to find the term successful ageing to be motivational, success being synonymous with performance and meeting expectations. However, workers over 60 years engaged in a discourse of natural bodily ageing as impacting performance, triggering discussions of curtailing or leaving paid work.

5.1 Who are we successfully ageing for, anyway?

My second participant, Deborah, a 53-year-old counsellor, had a strikingly adverse reaction to the term: she asked, 'Who are we successfully ageing for, anyway?' Deborah reacted to the term successful ageing with suspicion about how a qualitative assessment of her ageing body and identity might be used by her employer. Further, she rejected how workers in mid- to later life are potentially categorised into those who have successfully aged or not, and what this subjective categorisation might mean for how workers in mid- to later life are stereotyped at work. This reaction also encouraged discourse analysis of not only how participants reacted to successful ageing, but the words and emotions they used to do so. Deborah's quote is positioned at the beginning of this chapter to foreground the need to challenge the generally accepted use of 'successful ageing', whereby there are gains and losses (Baltes & Baltes, 1990), winners and losers (Strawbridge et al., 2002), and an assumption of freedom of personal agency (Truxillo et al., 2015; Carter, 2016).

> It's the word success that gets my alarm bells going . . . what does successful mean, anyway? . . . even the word ageing: do we have to use that word? Isn't it just about maturing? I don't know what it is, growing older, maturing, ageing, changing. . . . Successful ageing, nah, don't like that term very much, sorry [laughs] . . . part of me . . . is suspicious, if I am a person who is ageing successfully then I will be used by the working world. Business needs me to be a person who is ageing successfully so that I can support the economy. . . . I just, ugh: successful ageing says 'you're useful, but you're not'. No.

Deborah's sentiment not only raised a challenge to the term successful ageing, but also to who defines success and how success is measured in terms of the appearance, presentation and capability of the ageing body at work. Further, the word 'ageing' was challenged as that which carried a negative connotation at work. It would appear, then, that Deborah's assessment of successful ageing was as an inherently loaded and contradictory term. Conversely, Catherine, a 51-year-old counsellor, thought that the term successful ageing was 'meaningless in a way because it's so big', suggesting that the breadth and homogenous nature of successful ageing had actually rendered it irrelevant to individual workers. As mentioned in Chapter 3, the term 'older worker' also generated a strong reaction from some participants such as being 'mildly horrified to know that I'm regarded as the older workforce' (Julia, 50, teacher) and that I, as the researcher, 'ruffled some feathers' by using the term 'older workers' in the title of the study (Stella, 52, teacher). In response to the reaction of these participants to the nomenclature and discourse of successful ageing and the older worker, this chapter considers what successful ageing means to workers over 50 – the very individuals for whom it seeks to define.

5.2 Successful ageing: personal responsibility of healthy ageing

Healthy ageing was associated with successful ageing by all participants. Acknowledgement of chronological age and ageing bodies was articulated through an understanding of successful ageing as that which was earned from an agentic focus on the appearance of the healthily ageing body. Chronological age was viewed through a discourse of varied acceptance of relevance: 'it just doesn't matter what age you are' (Penny, 51), to full acceptance: 'just embracing your age' (Monica, 53) to it consciously not operating as a barrier to work: 'age won't be a barrier to me' (Georgina, 55). Despite this at times tentative acceptance of chronological age, the majority of participants discussed controlling the appearance of the ageing body as a condition to the acceptance of chronological age:

> Successful ageing would mean keeping fit and healthy . . . looking after yourself . . . . I never really bothered about [turning 50] because I feel the same . . . . I pretty much look the same in that I've not like put on weight or anything like that.
>
> (Stella, 52, teacher)

Appearance of healthy ageing was conveyed through an anti-chronological discourse, thus paradoxically not allowing for chronological age(ing). A discourse of halting time through 'keeping', 'staying' or 'remaining' healthy as relevant to the appearance of bodily ageing all spoke to work identity maintenance:

> keeping healthy, staying healthy . . . staying busy, staying energised . . . because that will be good for me.
>
> (Catherine, 51, counsellor)

> keeping fit, keeping well . . .
>
> (Monica, 53, nursery nurse)

The appearance of not looking older extended for many women in particular as not feeling old: successful ageing would be not feeling old, not looking around wondering, 'Oh, I feel so old!' (Julia, 50, teacher). The maintenance of the appearance of bodily ageing as that of an anti-chronological standpoint was associated with agentic behaviours by the individual in terms of self and work identity. Beyond maintenance and controlling the ageing body – or the appearance of not-old – was a discourse around youthfulness and staying young: healthy ageing as successful ageing was reflected by 'someone who stays young' (Rachel, 50), or 'trying to remain the same as you were when you were young . . . don't lose yourself' (Penny, 51).

Healthy ageing was also communicated through a discourse of energy, which was prevalent among both participants. Energy was associated with a desire for a youthful body, specifically the appearance of energy and was firmly associated with healthy ageing: 'having health but feeling healthy and still having energy . . . to do what I want' (Adele, 50, professor/medical doctor). The appearance of energy was exemplified by Kara, aged 62, who reported low energy due to lack of sleep and anxiety associated with natural bodily ageing: 'I think it shows in my face . . . the bags under my eyes and general feeling of tiredness . . . just don't have energy'. Energy was also seen as both controllable and uncontrollable by participants, as that which could be harnessed to keep up at work and conversely that which was depleted through work in direct comparison with younger colleagues:

> [I]t's hard to keep up . . . trying to keep energy levels and I think looking after yourself so that you can keep up . . .
>
> (Penny, 51, teacher)

The lack of allowance for chronological age through the anti-chronological discourse of not appearing older was viewed as effortful, yet controllable by the individual through agentic behaviours. Participants who presented themselves within a highly agentic personal narrative discussed controlling the appearance of the ageing body. Interestingly, these data presented themselves through a discourse which acted as a warning to others. For example, as previously reported, Rachel, a 50-year-old lawyer, said with regard to early exit from the labour force that

> people can age themselves. . . . People can persuade themselves that they are hard done by because they are female or they are hard done by because they are older, but actually are they performing to the best of their ability . . . they persuade themselves that they have to go'.

Similarly, Laura contradictorily warned women struggling with the appearance of bodily ageing through menopausal weight gain to maintain their weight, while trying to accept the 'menopausal belly':

> [I]t's all very well to sit and get fat and say that everybody else should be nice to me and give me a job, but [long pause]. . . . I wouldn't like to

> think that people are discriminated against because of it, but invariably they probably are, especially if it's a visual job. . . . I don't think it is healthy for women to let their weight go'.

This warning of looking older to others was further illustrated by Penny, a 51-year-old teacher, who personally stressed the irrelevance of chronological age, yet determined that successful ageing was to be found through a youthful looking body: 'it's quite sad, people who have let themselves go a bit and don't make much effort . . . '. This othering of advocacy to conceal the appearance of bodily ageing, while positioned as concern and consideration, could be viewed as perpetuating the socially constructed desire to appear youthful at work, thus potentially reinforcing the concept of an older worker who appears not to have aged at all (Rowe & Kahn, 2015). Here, participants themselves appeared to reinforce this message both through their own worker identity and to others within their same-sex peer group.

More frequently, however, was a discourse around the appearance of bodily ageing controlling work, work identity and attitudes around labour force participation. Healthy ageing was viewed by most to 'maintain your options and choices' while realising that 'some aspects of health you might not have any influence over' (Fran, 56, charity worker). This sense of requirement to achieve successful ageing was through controlling healthy ageing to work on the individual's own terms and not have the ageing body determine how and for how long the individual would continue to work:

> Successful ageing would be stopping work at a point when I felt I was ready to stop . . . not stopping because I felt worn out.
>
> (Julia, 50, teacher)

> I have to think very carefully about how much of the counselling work I do and what I balance it with, so that will determine how I work and how long I work.
>
> (Deborah, 53, counsellor)

Participants also discussed health issues that had been exacerbated by the nature of the job. These affected how participants were able to perform at work: the ageing body threatened their ability to work in future. More specifically, the impact of health issues, exacerbated by ageing within a specific work context, led to choices around early retirement and changing how work was done. There were a number of such examples from participant narratives, all highly contextual based on the nature of their health issues, the nature of their work, the flexibility and control they have over their work, and how financial and domestic situations enabled a way of working differently in future. Following are two extended quotes, both from teachers, about how individual perceptions of the appearance of bodily ageing and work-related health concerns were exacerbated by the nature of the job and reduced choice around later life working. These examples, while similar, demonstrate a nuanced individual experience of contextualised agency. I say that appearance of bodily ageing here as Julia's narrative was that of an awareness that she was seen not to be able to hear by students – her hearing was reflected through the physical discomfort of her body and actually having to lean in to her students, which she felt was an ageing gesture, within a noisy class environment. For Penny, it was the appearance (sound) of her voice changing with age:

> I had a diagnosis about 20 years ago of obscure auditory dysfunction . . . . I recognise that it is becoming harder for me to hear what I need to hear in the classroom . . . apparently, it's very common in teachers, because the environment in which we work tends to affect our hearing [long pause]. That's one aspect of my physical ageing that I can see having an impact on my job.
>
> (Julia, 50, teacher)

> Health is vital. I'm a singer. I've had surgery on my vocal chords, so I have to maintain health on my vocal chords or I can't work. Hearing is a big worry for music teachers, loud noises, quite a lot of musicians going deaf . . . so health-wise, in my job I have to be careful.
>
> (Penny, 51, teacher)

5.3 Successful ageing: economic ageing through perceptions of others

Economic ageing was presented as successful ageing through the ageing body being or perceived as being productive and 'useful' at work. Data provided evidence that identity work was engaged to promote the concept of the productive worker: economic ageing was a discursive identity conducted by participants, although job type differences were found. The key distinction between economic ageing and the previously discussed healthy ageing was found in answering the question of who (re)produces the notion and standards of successful ageing at work, specifically out-group others. Economic ageing was overwhelmingly valued through perceptions of others within the world of work. The following subsection presents two key themes of economic ageing as successful ageing. First, how the participant was perceived as a productive worker through the appearance of bodily ageing had a significant impact on how they positioned themselves at work. Second, the transitional nature of natural bodily ageing, combined with financial and domestic constraints affected a perceived threat to productively stay in work or extend working lives for women at work.

5.3.1 Keeping up: being perceived as a productive worker

The tentative acceptance of chronological age was in contradiction to the presentation of the ageing body as an economically productive body: economic ageing was effortful. Agentic behaviours of not 'letting' the chronologically older body appear older were enmeshed with an anti-chronological discourse of 'still' and 'maintaining' economic productivity at work as exemplified by Laura, 50:

> Successful ageing means that you are still working and productive in the economic sense and maintaining a certain degree of success in whatever area you work in.

The successfully ageing older worker was generally viewed as a productive worker. Further, data revealed that perceptions based on what we think others think about us worked to prioritise the productive worker as the benchmark for successfully ageing at work. For participants who welcomed or accepted the agentic appeal to maintain work performance through 'becoming' an older worker, there was a sense that as long as performance was sufficient, they would continue at work and their ageing bodies were not a cause for concern. However, participants who acknowledged or who were beginning to acknowledge a dissonance between the requirement of the job and their current or short-term future physical capacity appeared to have a self-awareness of 'knowing when to go' (Penny). This was balanced with fear of not meeting expectations around the standards inherently set by the job itself or through perceived expectations of others.

For example, the teaching profession seemed to be particularly susceptible to an incongruence between the physical requirements of the job, especially in terms of energy and the physical ability of the 'older' teacher: having to 'keep up' (Penny). Again, a narrative of fear of the ageing body constraining the worker to continue in their current role was driven by perceptions of out-group members. In Penny's case, it was how she perceived that primary-aged school children would perceive her as their teacher if she had the appearance of someone who was lacking in energy. Penny's sense of responsibility to her students was enhanced by her sense of work ethic, which was also reflected in Stella's narrative around performing at a certain level.

There was a sense of not being able to work: not being on her 'A game' (Stella) as a signal that the job was becoming too physically demanding. This perception of self was seen through the eyes of the students of these teachers – it was the appearance of bodily ageing which planted a seed of doubt as to whether they could maintain their current work performance until retirement. This directly affected retention and extension of work attitudes. While participants spoke of healthy ageing, the ability of the ageing body to be productive, to contribute to the organisation and to meet personal and organisational expectations at work was the focus of participant narrative:

> I'd be frightened I'd be tired, and wouldn't put enthusiasm into my lessons and they might pick up on that . . . you owe it to them to be at

> your best, not tired and old and grumpy and sore . . . you have to know when to go.
>
> (Penny, 51, teacher)

> I try to bring my A game all the time . . . and I feel I'm not on my A game . . . you're running around . . . up and down stairs a lot of the time. . . . I'll retire at 60, hopefully. (long pause) I don't think I would want to stop work though, so at 60 I might go part-time . . . I am feeling a bit jet lagged this session.
>
> (Stella, 52, teacher)

Participants also displayed a discourse focused on expectations of others at work: 'people who are performing in their 60s . . . at the same level as they have . . . and I don't notice any[thing] different at all' (Rachel, 50, lawyer). Again, this expectation did not allow for chronological age. The suggestion was that ageing bodies of workers in mid- to later life go relatively undetected if their performance is maintained at the level it was when they were a younger worker, thus not allowing the older worker to experience or display the natural and biological passage of time and of ageing.

While the discourse around healthy ageing was, as noted in the beginning of this chapter, person-centric, i.e. conducted and performed by the individual for the benefit of the individual, economic ageing was discussed as through perceptions of others, for the benefit of others, a 'body for others' (Cutcher & Achtel, 2017, citing Bourdieu, 1977). This discourse of performance and productivity reflected more of a two-way interplay (Beech, 2011) than the discourse of healthy ageing, which was more inside-out as a projection of self to others. For example, while chronological age was generally accepted by participants themselves, they were concerned about the perceptions of others at work around attribution of value to the older worker, or economic ageing. Further, even with the tentative acceptance of chronological age, a discourse of fear related to perceived reduction in economic capabilities in a future of work emerged. Georgina summarised this concept of the contradiction between self-acceptance of chronological age and concerns about perceptions of the economic ability of her older body, both now and in the future of work. Her explicit articulation that perceptions mattered more than reality highlighted the power of perceptions in how workers in mid- to later life engaged with intentions to work in later life:

> [S]uccessful ageing means to me that my age won't be a barrier to me living the kind of life I want to lead . . . for me, that would be around other people's perceptions of my capabilities rather than mine, I don't feel that there are any limitations on my ability at the moment, I'm relatively young aged, I suppose [laughs]. I don't know if I'll feel the same in 10 years' time . . . maybe when I become older, and frail . . . I might

> find that I'm more tired or my body hurts but for me I think it would be around perceptions more than reality.
>
> (Georgina, 55, director)

Perceptions of out-group others were seemingly required by some participants to validate their economic contribution to work. More explicitly, favourable perceptions of others at work were actively sought to validate the economic contribution of workers in mid- to later life. Their own abilities were not in question, but an acknowledgement of others was required to be seen as a valuable, respected and experienced worker:

> [I'm] still feeling that I have plenty to offer, wanting to be respected and seen as experienced by other people.
>
> (Catherine, 51, counsellor)

As discussed earlier in this chapter, healthy ageing was displayed through an energetic discourse. A discourse of energy also presented itself as the vehicle to display an appearance of a youthful body as a productive worker. Participant narrative around energy and being tired was generally defeatist and suggested a direct association with intentions to work in later life. Physical changes in energy levels were not directly visible; however, the impact of low energy on bodily appearance was interpreted by participants has having direct implications on how they were seen at work. For example, Georgina said she felt that the onus was on the individual worker to 'convince' their employer that energy levels had been maintained as those of younger workers, equating this with observable attributes, i.e. skills. A combination of actual impact on performance, perception of lowered performance and unwillingness to continue with current work demands was also attributed to how the appearance of lowered energy due to an ageing body might be interpreted by the employer. Participants spoke to the physical appearance of looking tired (reduced energy), which, for Laura, was met with the perceived accusation of looking in some way incorrect or incongruent with expectations. The gendered appearance of energy was associated with employer and colleague perceptions and potential age and/or gender discrimination – participants felt a punitive action against looking tired at work. Successful ageing was equated with hiding or masking signs of bodily ageing:

> I imagine you become less attractive to employers, unless you keep your skill set up to date and you can convince them that your energy levels are the same, you're not allowed to discriminate overtly are you? But I bet you that doesn't stop it from happening . . .
>
> (Georgina, 55, director)

> [A] lot of women at work who say they've had a bad night sleep, certainly into the peri-menopausal age, there's no allowance for that at

> work if you look tired . . . it's always you look tired as some kind of accusation that you shouldn't be looking tired . . . and I think maybe women get a bit more of that than men, women get commented on about how tired they look a bit more, maybe it's more obvious in women in their face, bags . . . .
>
> (Laura, 50, teacher)

Participants over 60 years of age discussed natural health decline as a catalyst to change how they performed work. The distinction between healthy and economic ageing was more blurred for workers over 60. These older participants appeared to personally identify their health complaints through their self-identity, not as their worker identity, representing a distance or separation of self. The narrative of worker identity tended to shift from successful ageing as productive worker to a coping worker:

> Making the most of yourself as you age, doing the best you can I suppose for what you're doing and what age you are . . . . Coping with what is expected of you . . . .
>
> (Orla, 62, nursery nurse)

While all participants in this age group presented with health complaints, it appeared that natural bodily ageing was more impactful on their day-to-day ability to perform to expectations at work. For example, Evelyn, aged 61, recently changed jobs from cleaner to receptionist to accommodate the fatigue associated with natural bodily ageing: 'I'm more tired when I go home . . . . I'd say it's more ageing rather than the illness'. Similarly, Kara, a 62-year-old secretary, referred to arthritis in her hands, directly attributing the condition to work: 'probably exacerbated . . . because I type, it's uncomfortable . . . apart from being slower . . . other than that, I don't have any major issues'.

Participants who were closer to retirement also discussed their ageing bodies in relation to choices around their planned exit from the labour force. Control was not simply a matter of controlling the ageing body; for both participants, their choice to stay at work was attributed to financial and domestic constraints, exemplified by Kara, who is unable to retire for another six years despite a deep bodily fatigue due to natural bodily ageing not ill-health: 'I should have retired at 60 . . . successful ageing at work is being retired at this age'.

Some participants referred to financial constraints due to domestic contexts, mainly divorce, as the reason behind extending their working lives either up to or even beyond SPA. This was, however, contingent upon coping with both the ageing body at work, as well as organisational expectations of others. Other participants demonstrated a choice around working longer due to their financial and domestic situation. These participants viewed successful ageing differently, for example:

> I think successful ageing is doing all sorts of things to keep positive . . . . I personally feel quite positive about the next stage.
>
> (Natalie, 60, administrator – three months away from early retirement to adopt a full-time carer role).

Participants also engaged in behaviours to mitigate the appearance of an ageing body and were reluctant to report health conditions to their employer due to an uncertainty as to whether they would accommodate an ageing body at work. The fear of exposing the appearance of bodily ageing at work was represented by Orla, a 62-year-old nursery nurse who experienced recurring pain from a hip condition, which acted to restrict certain forms of movement, specifically sitting for too long – or as Orla put it, 'Would they be willing to let me away with that . . . ? ,' in relation to a request to stand rather than sit.

It was interesting to note that a number of participants blamed the sedentary nature of their job for poor health outcomes associated with the appearance of bodily ageing, including weight due to sedentary job. This exemplified by Isla, aged 58: 'I'm unhealthy because I put the demands of my job before what my body needed . . . not moving around, sitting at your desk, missing lunch . . . '.

5.4 Chapter discussion

Organisation and management literature and much of the policy established around workers in mid- to later life has ubiquitously adopted successful ageing to describe workers in mid- to later life as economically productive members of the labour force, as workers who have something to offer society (Riach & Loretto, 2009), which is an inherently positive outlook. Expanding on this concept of the ideal worker, a within-person contradiction of 'be older, but don't look it' presented itself through two mechanisms of identity work around the ageing body: healthy ageing and economic ageing. Both healthy and economic ageing involved positively contributing to work, while resisting physical signs of ageing; however, they did so through different approaches to identity work and liminal practices.

Findings present the novel inclusion of not only self-perceptions but perceptions of others (Carlson et al., 2011; Meister et al., 2017) in how successful ageing is understood and internalised by the worker (see Figure 5.1 for summary of chapter findings).

Economic ageing, more than healthy ageing, was overwhelmingly valued through the eyes of others with the world of work, highlighting the role of perceptions of others and how this identity work relinquishes power over the self to others. Workers appeared to agentically support a broader narrative

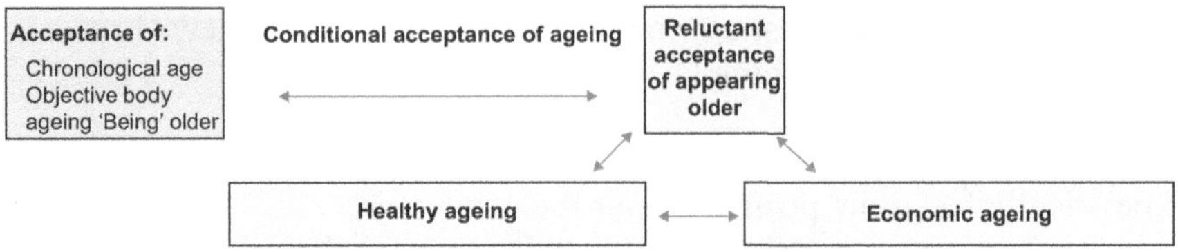

Source of influence	Self-perception, personal responsibility	Perceptions of others
Identity work: dialogic construction and liminal identity work (Beech, 2011)	Inside-out initiation. Seeking maintenance of self. Reflection of self against youthful model of older. Threat of internalised ageism from self.	Two-way interplay. Recognition of ageing, reflection of ageing stereotypes, threat of internalism ageism from others.
Liminality (Ibarra & Obodaru, 2016; Turner, 1969)	Self-guided process. Culturally problematic narrative, seeking socially legitimate narrative.	Highly institutionalised ritual, guided by elders where possible, otherwise guided by social construction of the appearance of older.
Themes	Bodily ageing: performance of healthy ageing Successful ageing earned through agentic control over appearance of bodily ageing Energetic discourse: *Keep up* Anti-chronological discourse: halting time Warning to peers: *Don't let yourself go* Menopause: uncontrollable challenge to successful ageing	Effortful display of productivity levels Maintenance of performance reduces salience of looking older: *Be on your A game all the time* Perceived as productive worker: *Keep up* Seeking value through the eyes of out-group others <60 years focus on performance; >60 on coping Early exit decisions based on appearance-related performance perceptions: *Know when to go*

Figure 5.1 Chapter 5 findings overview

whereby being older was associated with the threat of economic redundancy; however, rather than age being the limiting factor (Trethewey, 2000), it was the appearance of ageing that was associated with a threat to economic ageing as successful ageing. An individual's value and investment in their own bodies as a source of labour in light of perceived economic value is a common thread in research on aesthetic labour, which is highly gendered (Warhurst & Nickson, 2007). While women did experience differences in how perceptions of self and others informed their identity work around economic ageing, job and industry type and age appeared to be influential on work outcomes.

Healthy ageing was a narrative engaged by all but one participant in this study, reinforcing findings that health is a significant barrier to continued employment for workers in mid- to later life and ill health is a 'push factor' to early exit (Edge et al., 2017; Winkelmann-Gleed, 2012). Identity work was conducted to maintain the appearance of health, fitness and energy, attempting to control the inevitable ageing of the gendered body through combination of healthy, active, harmonious and productive ageing (Carpentieri et al., 2016), and through the association of positive health and youthful appearance (Carter, 2016; Cameron et al., 2019). In accordance with successful ageing literature, findings here support the expectation of neo-liberal attitudes and personal responsibility towards successful ageing and managing one's own appearance of ageing at work (Cameron et al., 2019; Zacher, 2015).

The appearance of bodily ageing appeared to stem from the social construct of 'beauty as youthful', which conveys to women in mid- to later life more than men to associate ageing with bodily sagging, wrinkles, grey hair, weight and posture changes (Cameron et al., 2019; Hurd Clarke & Griffin, 2008; Hurd Clarke, 2010) resulting in adverse social and economic outcomes (Bowman et al., 2016). Appearing not-old through healthy ageing was dominated by a self-serving and self-motivated discourse, exemplified by Catherine: 'because that will be good for me'. Presentation of a youthful body through individual agentic behaviours was assessed against the slightly younger self, in line with previous research finding that a youthful aesthetic is more important for women than men (Cameron et al., 2019; Trethewey, 1999). Bodily anxiety was demonstrated by women who spoke about tension between strong neo-liberal accountability to be seen as healthily ageing and still 'needing' to be recognisable as feminine and youthful (Carter, 2016).

Further, there were apparent penalties for those who did not make the 'effort' to maintain health, reinforcing a blame culture (Emirbayer & Johnson, 2008), which was seemingly perpetuated by the workers themselves. This othering of health advocacy was conducted within same-sex peer groups. This was exemplified by warnings such as 'don't lose yourself' and 'it's not healthy for women to let their weight go', despite the natural biological cause of weight gain for menopause-aged women. This also resonated with findings around healthism (Carter, 2016; Powroznik, 2017): participants were aware that they might face value-based judgements based on an unhealthy appearance. It should be noted that participant narrative of keeping and staying fit and healthy assumes that participants are generally fit and well, showing the relatively privileged position of these participants.

Participants conducted identity work to foreground their 'healthy ageing', a separation from their health concern or unhealthy aspect of their ageing body, thus creating a dissonance or a separation of self. Individuals inherently work towards resolving dissonance (Petriglieri, 2011; McMullin & Cairney, 2004; Gray & Kish-Gephart, 2013; Alvesson et al., 2008); however, here we have an active and performative separation of self, based on the perception of health and its perceived value within the world of work. An example of this was the menopausal body. Menopause was revealed as an uncontrollable aspect of gendered bodily ageing, whereby identity work was conducted to 'endure' or 'minimise' the appearance of symptoms. Emerging literature suggests that menopause management can be addressed through promotion of 'healthy ageing' and improved physical work environments (Hardy et al., 2018; Hickey et al., 2017; Jack et al., 2016); however, data here represented menopause as an uncontrollable challenge to actual and the appearance of healthy ageing.

Answering the research question of from whom do workers in mid- to later life draw perceptions, it was clear that participants themselves drew on stereotypes of workers in mid- to later life as less adaptable and less competent than younger workers (Gordon & Arvey, 2004), less productive (McMullin &

Cairney, 2004) and as peripheral and disposable labour (Loretto & White, 2006). These behaviours and experiences arguably worked to self-reinforce internalised ageism. While these arguably outdated stereotypes (Ng & Feldman, 2012) formed the basis of perceptions around their economic ageing, participant narratives were of themselves as workers within their industry, without significant reference to gender. The only gendered narrative within economic ageing was around the impact of menopause on energy, which was obviously directly impactful for women and not men. Further, participants in this study displayed aspects of ageing anxiety, which was behind identity work. This supports previous findings that ageing anxiety not only affects one's own perceptions of ageing (Carter, 2016), but that those who experienced ageing anxiety themselves were more likely to stereotype based on age or avoid those of a similar age (Shaw & Langman, 2017).

Both health and economic productivity were discussed in terms of the future appearance and capabilities of the ageing body. The ageing body threatened ability to work in the future, thus creating a barrier to continued labour force participation. There was a broad sense of the ageing body being unpredictable in future due to general decline. Researchers of successful ageing suggest that agentic workers in mid- to later life are more likely to focus on future opportunities (Zacher, 2013), while a future time perspective suggests that individual time horizons affect the resources that an employee might invest in goal-oriented behaviours (Carstensen, 2006). Further, recent identity research found that negative identity work by younger workers was adopted to render the present less important, instead focusing on a future work identity, which challenged the assumption that identity work is used primarily to convey a positive sense of self (Brown, 2015). Findings here support workers deprioritising the present through negative identity work, but the future of these workers felt precarious, in line with future time perspective (Carstensen, 2006), potentially leading workers to agentically foreground their former selves as healthier and more productive workers.

This chapter was in part motivated by Deborah's challenge of 'Who are we successfully ageing for, anyway?' Successful ageing is presented in the literature as a concept of aspiration of both employee and employer (Abraham & Hansson, 1995; Zacher, 2015). Despite previous recognition that organisations 'need to help employees develop throughout their careers' (Gibson & Barron, 2003), there remains a question over the responsibility of career development resting with the individual or organisation. Deborah's was a minority voice in the participant group who challenged why their agentic labour are being utilised by the organisation without their support. Successful ageing sets workers up to compete in the labour force where there are gains and losses (Baltes & Baltes, 1990), and winners and losers (Strawbridge et al., 2002). Further, successful ageing relies on an assumption of personal agency (Truxillo et al., 2015; Carter, 2016). This chapter confirms that personal agency is harnessed through identity work in order to achieve or at least be perceived as achieving successful ageing. However, if successful ageing is a motivation at work as findings support in this chapter, there was a concern raised that employers would adopt this personal agency and use it for their own purposes. This suggestion raises ethical questions about how employers might capitalise on the fact that workers in mid- to later life appear to be personally motivated by the concept and social construct of successful ageing as healthy ageing and/or economic ageing.

While agentic efforts of the workers are clearly of benefit to themselves in terms of work performance, progression, remuneration and retention, there is also undoubtedly a direct benefit to the employer of having employees who agentically and with effort work to stay healthy and economically viable and productive. Yet, it appears from these findings that workers place the burden on themselves with limited expectation of assistance in the process of ageing at work from the employer. This potentially provides a situation whereby the older body becomes a form of organisational asset and the value of the asset is recognised by the organisation, whereas the burden of its maintenance is recognised by the bearer.

The paradox appears to be that employees should believe that employers assist their ageing at work, and yet workers in mid- to later life do not want to be seen as older – especially in the eyes of younger colleagues and other important out-groups. The challenge for organisations is to manage and invest in older workers, enabling them to successfully age without the stigma of defining them as 'older' while spreading the benefits between employee and employer. Some scholars reject and rally against this form of neo-liberalism, calling for researchers to reject ideas of individualism which mask the role of agency or personal responsibility in a blame culture (Emirbayer & Johnson, 2008). Regardless of such opposition, the successful ageing concept is adopted in research without adequate challenge to what the headline term itself means to workers themselves; hence, the value and contribution of these findings.

6 Navigating the 'older worker' label through perceptions of ageing

In the previous two chapters, we have seen that becoming older through the natural progression of chronological age or the changing appearance of gendered bodily ageing is experienced differently depending on a range of factors including control over work, confidence, job type and emotional responses to the ageing body. It is the aim of this chapter to explore participant experiences of the transition of becoming older, whereby 50 years of age is generally accepted as 'older' in academic studies (Zacher, 2015), policy work (e.g. Altmann, 2015) and workplace supports (ageuk.org.uk/Scotland), seemingly without challenge. Further, this chapter provides a nuanced extension to theories of perception (Carlson et al., 2011) by answering the research questions around the source (who) and mechanisms (how) women in mid- to later life draw on perceptions of self and others to internalise ageism and participate in paid labour. Data revealed the ubiquitous presence of the intersection of age and gender in identity work, addressing the call for further enquiry into how gendered ageing interacts with contemporary work contexts (Riach et al., 2015).

This chapter is presented through three sub-themes, which demonstrate how – through identity work – participants adopted perceptions to connect with others, to be stereotyped by others, to be managed by others and to present themselves to others. Analysis suggested that self-perceptions follow a self-guided process of liminality through a largely experimental dialogic construction of identity work. However, identity work appeared to be highly institutionalised, operating through reflection processes of self-questioning identity construction through what was undoubtedly a changing situation (Beech, 2011; Ibarra & Obodaru, 2016). Findings are discussed at the end of this chapter.

6.1 Acceptance and rejection of an 'older worker' identity

Participants reported different emotive responses to the ageing body through being labelled as 'older'. As was outlined in Chapter 4, even the term 'older worker' in relation to people over 50 'ruffled some feathers' during the participant recruitment process. Clearly, the ubiquitous term of older worker

DOI: 10.4324/9781003439257-6

used by organisations, government and academics had not resonated with many participants. This section provides evidence of three reactions to the older worker label in relation to bodily ageing: rejection, willing acceptance and reluctant acceptance. Identity work was conducted by participants through liminal practices in relation to how this label resonated with their worker identity. This section also considers participant response to their bodies being judged and mandated as older through the label 'older worker' and the potential transitional nature of becoming older simply by being chronologically older than 50 years.

6.1.1 Rejection of an older worker identity

The appearance of healthy bodily ageing was a reason for rejection of the older worker label. A youthful appearance enabled rejection of an unwanted older worker identity. For example, Stella, a 52-year-old teacher, acknowledged that acceptance of the label might have been inevitable had the appearance of her body reflected her chronological age. As such, a youthful appearance enabled rejection of chronological age and associated categorisations:

> I pretty much look the same in that I've not like put on weight or anything like that . . . if I was substantially different now from how I was when I was 20, I might feel different about it . . . I don't feel that 50 has been a thing.

Identity work to reject the older worker label was also enabled through perceptions of others. Important others at work, in terms of the influence of meta-perceptions, tended to be out-group members rather than same-sex peers. For example, adopting chronological age as an anchor, a comparison of self with others appeared to be a crucial aspect of the influence of meta-perceptions. For example, Isla talked about how her younger line manager did not differentiate between Isla, aged 58, and her 38-year-old female colleague. This perception of inclusion, through a form of age-blindness, empowered Isla to reject the older worker label because 'We're treated exactly the same way. I never feel any different'. This was further exemplified by Natalie, a 60-year-old secretary, who through inclusion by and respect from her younger colleagues never felt like her ageing body was interpreted as a distinction at work and said she is 'never treated like I'm an old fuddy-duddy or whatever'. Further, Natalie echoed the sentiment of a number of participants whose own perception of an older worker was someone who was significantly older than themselves. She also pushed back on the ownership of the term older worker as not only not-hers but of my (the researcher's) construct and creation:

> he's 72, so he'd definitely be an older worker, but I don't class myself as that . . . your older worker is someone beyond the pension barrier, I think.

It was interesting to note that age-blindness, i.e. not treating age differently, was experienced positively by participants, whereas age equality initiatives generally encourage supporting different ages according to their needs.

6.1.2 *Willing acceptance of an older worker identity*

Interestingly, there was evidence of a within-person contradiction from two of the participants who clearly reflected a rejection of the older worker label, as previously detailed. However, as exemplified below by Natalie and Rachel, identity work was conducted to willingly accept the label of older worker. For example, Natalie reported a benefit in terms of appearance of age giving her 'an edge' over younger colleagues, while Rachel admitted to an evolving role identity as her team 'mum', as reported in Chapter 5. From a broader participant narrative, it appeared that these aspects of worker identity were experimental in that they were new to that individual:

> I quite like being the older person at work . . . . I think it gives me an edge.
>
> (Natalie, 60 administrator)

> I quite liked turning 50 . . . . I feel wise. I've got people in my team just now who are like 24, 25 and their mums are younger than me, so I feel like I'm their mum . . . I love that, 'cause they are like my little chicks [laughs].
>
> (Rachel, 50, lawyer)

Participants were also willing to accept being older due to the reality of chronological age: 'I don't mind it because I am an older worker' (Orla, 62, nursery nurse) and 'Can't get away from it. It's fine; it doesn't bother me' (Penny, 51, teacher). Willing acceptance of being older at work was also viewed as an opportunity for identity reinvention:

> Oh, I loved it, I loved turning 50 . . . . I thought I'm going to embrace it . . . so I kind of feel that you are reinventing yourself in your 50s – this is a good decade.
>
> (Monica, 53, nursery nurse)

6.1.3 *Reluctant acceptance of an older worker identity*

A similar number of participants reluctantly accepted the term older worker. Some expressed surprise by the term 'older worker' as being actively used to define and describe workers over 50 years of age: 'I'm surprised that 50 is classed as older' (Julia, 50, teacher). The chronological age of 50, for some participants, was a source of anxiety and a signpost of potential physical decline. Of the participants who displayed a reluctant acceptance of the older worker label, only one participant (Isla) felt that turning 50 was an immediate catalyst, a surprise event: 'turning 50 was a big thing for me, 'cause I suddenly thought, I'm 50? What happened?'. The other participants who reported a reluctant acceptance of ageing and being labelled as older at work did so through a gradual dawning or processing of understanding of what older meant to them. This sentiment was evidenced by the following quotes from participants who 'battled' the 'upheaval' of changing role identity, physical changes of an ageing body, seeing themselves as matching their previous perception of older and even not wanting to recognise themselves as older. For these participants, the older worker label presented a liminal state of transition without a clear resolution.

> I suppose it was a bit gradual, but I started looking into it a bit from 48 or 49 . . . I battled with the getting into 50 thing, not as a number or anything like that, but the physical changes . . . .
>
> (Laura, 50, teacher)

> I feel like I'm entering now a time of great change and upheaval . . . of changing my role . . . from being caregiver, nurturer, family . . . [long pause]. Now I'm faced with what is one's role going to be as you get older. What am I faced with in terms of physical changes as well as my appearance?
>
> (Adele, 50, doctor)

> I tend not to want to recognise the fact that I'm 30 years older than the person sitting beside me.
>
> (Deborah, 53, counsellor)

Within this described participant narrative and discourse, we saw glimpses of how the rejection or acceptance – both willing and reluctant – were formed and presented through perceptions of both the self and of others at work. The rest of this chapter delves more deeply into an analysis of the role of perception in identity work, highlighting who has the influence and control to label and (re)construct an older worker identity.

6.2 Self-perceptions of bodily ageing

Participants explicitly referred to appearing 'natural'; however, they admitted that the appearance of their ageing bodies required more effort to align with the desired worker identity as youthful or at least not-old. For example, Deborah, aged 53, referred to the necessity of change in body work as identity work to prevent her appearance of looking 'haggard and wiry and dry' or 'knackered', to the extent of acknowledging a partial loss of self and also aiming to appear age-appropriate:

> I used to have ringlets, lots of ringlets and I feel like that part of me has gone . . . . I wouldn't want to pretend that I'm not making any changes . . . the thing about growing older is that I can't really get away

> with being that wild about it, or that natural . . . . So, I do put eye liner on in a way that I didn't used to.

This broadly held sentiment of increased and focused effort was evidenced through a narrative of body work as identity work to manage a youthful appearance. This was conducted by other participants who spoke through a discourse of self-perception and self-efficacy of appearance:

> . . . as you get older you have to put more effort in . . . . I dye my hair and stuff perhaps I shouldn't be bothered about [because] I'd be grey otherwise . . . .
>
> (Georgina, 55, director)

> Make-up has become more important to me as I've got older . . . . I wear make-up every day now, I didn't used to . . . . I don't consciously associate it with menopause, but it has happened around that time.
>
> (Catherine, 51, counsellor)

This was further exemplified by Laura, who spoke of maintaining a sense of self through appearing attractive, although through her own admission was 'trying to get her head around' how to combine her desire to retain the appearance of 'sexy' with an ageing body:

> . . . an effort in appearance . . . self-preservation, I suppose . . . and just making an effort with everything . . . the older sexy woman thing . . . 'cause I don't think we should hang up our sexiness and our appeal and our attraction once we hit like 45.
>
> (Laura, 50, teacher)

This within-person dissonance between wanting to appear natural and wanting their appearance to conform to the social construct of what an attractive-older-woman 'should' look like was epitomised by Deborah. She exemplified the shame, resentment and effort required in fighting the natural process of ageing and in presenting her notion of a socially acceptable ageing female body at work:

> . . . the number of friends I have who haven't put on weight post-menopause are few and far between. It just seems like a natural process actually that I don't really want to fight. I'm slightly ashamed of fighting it. The feminist in me says, whoa, this is a natural process (long pause) let it be. But equally society says women should be thin, (pause) that's the message, everywhere, all of the time . . . . This takes a lot more effort that I ever used to have to put into it . . . . I'm resentful at having to spend that time.
>
> (Deborah, 53, counsellor)

There was only one exception from the women who presented a narrative of self-perception of appearance. Stella, a 52-year-old teacher, had previously experimented with wearing make-up and grooming at work to 'dress up' as she turned 50; however, more recently, she had a sense that students preferred to see her make-up free and looking 'natural'. She referred to her experiments of make-up as her 'teacher face', which she rejected in relation to her teenage students, who she felt had a desire for an authentic appearance, suggesting the influence of perceptions of others:

> I don't have a work face . . . . I remember when I first started teaching, I tried to put on a teacher face . . . this is exhausting, how can I do this, and then I thought actually – the kids like it when you are congruent . . . . I am who I am, wherever I am.

Self-stereotyping based on their ageing bodies at work was presented as a form of internalised gendered ageism in response to a perceived, intersectional stigma around perceptions of age and gender at work.

> I would be lying if I wasn't conscious of the fact that I look at the mirror and think you're looking older and how can I stop that happening . . . for men, it can be seen as a positive, there's still that stigma around women [in mid- to later life] . . . .
>
> (Georgina, 55)

> . . . women put on weight as they get older, but we should be allowed to do that without any stigma.
>
> (Laura, 50)

As we have seen, self-perceptions can lead to within-person contradiction of authenticity due to a dissonance between gendered identity ideals that do not allow for the appearance of ageing. While we have seen that identity work conducted through appearance-related self-perceptions were largely formed through a comparison with our younger selves, what is unclear is to what extent other influencers play a role. Deborah's following quote spoke to this concept of looking beyond the self and self-perceptions for influences over how women in mid- to later life experience bodily ageing, demonstrating the role of how others perceive the older worker – or more specifically, meta-perceptions, or how participants perceived they were perceived by out-group others.

> I don't know how much of [fearing looking older] is self-imposed, and how much of that is imposed by the people around me . . . if you don't impose it on yourself, you're less likely to invite that from others.

6.3 Meta-perceptions of ageing at work

Meta-perceptions are individual understandings of self, based on how an individual understands that they themselves are noticed, recognised and understood by 'others' (Meister et al., 2014). Themes in this section each reflect a nuanced gendered approach to understanding the gendered ageing body at work, highlighting the source of influence and control, and the mechanisms behind identity work which potentially affect how women in mid- to later life work.

Some participants suggested that their appearance of ageing provided a connection with younger colleagues. However, this was a tenuous connection contingent upon an optimal perceived age difference, positioning the participant in a liminal position of not-too-old and not-too-young. There were a number of mechanisms through which perceptions of out-group others were understood by participants.

Connections were made with younger out-group members whereby the ageing body was presented within acceptable differential parameters, old enough to be older, but not-too-old. This was exemplified by Catherine, aged 51: 'Particular groups of clients were connecting with me . . . the perception was that I didn't look so old that the younger people couldn't connect with me . . . '. This finding of looking the 'right age' to make a meaningful connection was contingent upon the age profile of the out-group, more so than gender, although gender certainly was relevant. A lack of connection with younger colleagues was assumed due to perceptions of looking significantly older, moving beyond that 'sweet spot' of relative age difference:

> . . . so, I still feel about 28, vivacious, attractive, and clearly, I look like an ancient old bat to most of them [younger colleagues] . . . .
>
> (Adele, 50, doctor)

Out-group influence and control was relevant to job type. For teachers, influence was held by students, which appeared to be a non-gendered connection, whereas for counsellors, influence was held by clients, whereby both age and gender were intersectionally relevant. The office workers spoke about younger colleagues and/or male colleagues, but never same-sex peers. This lack of connection was brought about through a comparison between young versus old, younger versus older, and the older body compared with the younger body of out-group members. The connection was deemed essential to effectively perform the job in line with previous performance levels, directly contributing to attitudes of work retention:

> . . . teenagers think that we are all aged anyway and don't necessarily make a difference between those of us in our 50s and those in our 30s . . . to them we are all decrepit . . . . I think there is a point where it would just get harder to relate to teenagers . . . if you cannot relate to them, you cannot teach them.
>
> (Julia, 50, teacher)

> I don't want to work until I'm an aged old lady and the children are rolling their eyes . . . us teachers have to think what else can we do.
>
> (Penny, 51, teacher)

A lone voice suggested that connections with out-group members were neither positive or negative to older worker identity, 'just different', and were dependent upon how the individual out-group member related to her. In Monica's case, she was talking about her younger students:

> . . . some [students] will treat you the same as the younger [staff] because they think everyone is old . . . others will treat you like a granny. It's just different.

The majority of participants displayed a general awareness of stereotypes relating to women in mid- to later life. These stereotypes were broadly based around expectations of productivity and performance. Perceptions around stereotypes were understood through the eyes of exclusively out-group members, with a lack of participant narrative around judgements from same-sex peers. In fact, Adele referred to the 'sisterhood getting stronger as you get older' in opposition to her meta-perceptions of similar-age men and younger colleagues. Data provide evidence of who women in mid- to later life might turn to for these perceptions, engaging in liminal practices of self-questioning and repositioning of worker identity:

> . . . you're definitely perceived like you might not know the answer.
> (Penny, 51)

While the majority of participants discussed stereotyping by others within their current roles, age stereotyping in their current organisations was also relevant to the recruitment process. Meta-perceptions around stereotypes of age as physical decline or unhealthy ageing acted as a barrier to perceived success at job interviews, even suggesting that meta-perceptions were a barrier to attending job interviews. This finding was exemplified by Laura, age 50:

> We face this stuff that we never thought we would, you know, going to an interview and lining up, looking your best then going ach, [long pause] because we know that they're going to be thinking, oh she's going to be off with this, or oh she's going to be . . . .

Stereotyping by younger colleagues appeared to reinforce the concept of 'age as decline' in performance around speed, creativity, task flexibility and general competence:

> . . . you can feel a bit undermined sometimes . . . [younger staff] think you won't be able to do it, or you're not fast enough, so they do it for you like you're old and can't manage. I hate it; it's like, how dare you?
> (Penny, 51)

> . . . people do tend to think that you're not going to be as quick with information technology . . . you're not as creative, you're not as flexible.

> I do think there's still all those perceptions around workers [in mid- to later life]. [long pause] And I can remember having them myself when I was younger, so don't really know what to do about it.
>
> (Fran, 56 administrator)

Fran made an interesting point in terms of no obvious solution through an awareness that her younger self perpetrated and engaged in age stereotyping, suggesting a perception that age stereotyping has insufficiently changed over the previous decades. In addition to younger colleagues and students, a small number of women felt age and gender discrimination through perceptions of 'sexist issues and attitudes of some of my senior male colleagues at the time' (Georgina). Adele exemplified this further referring to her understanding of the mechanism behind appearance and age-related judgements, which was relevant to the evolutionary aspect of the relationship and dynamics of control between women:

> The invisibility of going into your 50s. I think women have more or less treated me the same. I think men have treated me differently, which is a fairly predictable one in that when you are younger, you still look like you might be able to have their babies, they treat you rather nicely and now they treat you like you don't exist . . . . If a bunch of middle-aged men aren't interested to listen, well, then I couldn't give a damn.
>
> (Adele, 50, doctor)

6.4 'Dress your age'

Participants generally viewed attire and grooming as an integral part of their work identity. The majority of participants referred to attire as the means to 'dress your age', which had two clear and distinct meanings. First, participants approached attire as the responsibility to dress their ageing body in a way that it looked as though an effort had been made and to avoid dated age-stereotyped models of how women in mid- to later life present themselves through attire. Second, participants referred to attire as a way to identify with or present an identity of what they personally deemed as 'contextually appropriate' for perceptions around their age (both chronological and subjective), job type and role seniority. Dressing your age as a concept, through both of its key themes presented here, created an authenticity paradox (Ibarra, 2015), whereby participants who were seeking the contextually appropriate and assuming a personal responsibility appeared to struggle with a sense of betraying their real selves or natural identities. This authenticity paradox created a liminal space in which individuals engaged in liminal identity work (Beech, 2011), or identity work of liminal practices.

Further, the two key themes within 'dress your age' presented a common causal or explanatory thread: there appeared to be a lack of role models in how the older body should be presented, be dressed and be displayed in terms of masculinity and femininity at work. A further common thread between these two themes was identity work, which was conducted as a form of impression management not necessarily as looking younger, but against looking old or older. I provide evidence of an authenticity paradox, finishing with examples of identity work conducted within the liminal space created by this authenticity paradox.

Identity work appeared to be based on an arguably outdated image of 'older', whereby speculative or experimental identity work was an adaptive strategy: 'most of investment into themselves is only to stop things from becoming worse' (Skeggs, 1997).

Identity work was to mitigate being perceived as older rather than looking younger. Laura (50, teacher) said, 'I don't want to become a fleece-wearing-stomp-around-the-country person, I like getting dressed up and feeling nice and going to work.': her sense was that different clothes from those she enjoyed wearing would convey an unwanted image. Further, a number of participants drew upon a gendered and arguably outdated narrative to describe their fears of dressing older. Catherine, a 51-year-old counsellor, warned 'don't get fuddy-duddy, don't cross over into the frumpy camp', but her attire choices had to balance with not looking too young: 'I'm looking for something younger than 50, but not mutton dressed as lamb'. Deborah, a 53-year-old counsellor reiterated this sentiment – 'it's the word fuddy-duddy that I avoid', which she enacted by consciously wearing designer clothes, making a point that the label was seen by her younger colleagues and clients, 'so there is a consciousness in wearing the [brand of sportswear] leggings and an eye to fashion'. This importance of the opinion of others extended to the teachers in this study, summarised by Laura, aged 50, who reflected on the importance her students' opinions:

> I don't want them to say Oh, Miss [name] used to dress lovely, but now she's just sitting there like an old frump . . . there's an association with the old frump, which is against women.

This aspect of presentation was also reported beyond the individual to an expectation of others at work, which was objectively represented by Rachel (50, lawyer):

> I would discourage people from being dowdy at work, in the interests of relevance and professionalism.

What was interesting to note here was that these participants appeared to acknowledge a transitional phase of 'becoming older' and actively engaged in identity work to avoid perceptions associated with ageing. The discourse was relatively old-fashioned – 'frump'; 'fuddy-duddy'. By adopting this outdated model in their own minds, these women actively worked to repel their version of an ageing identity. Without clear role models or guide as to what they should adopt as appropriate work attire for their female sex-type jobs, there was a default to appeal to what their younger students might approve of (Laura) or to model or mimic younger clients in an effort to connect with them (Deborah) or simply to look age-appropriate (Natalie), thus negotiating a transitional identity of 'older' within the expectations of perceptions of out-group members.

> People are often saying to me that I don't look as old as I am . . . . I'm not quite sure . . . whether or not they would react differently to me if they thought I was as old as I am . . . .
>
> (Deborah, 53, counsellor)

> There are definitely things you can't wear anymore . . . . I wouldn't do plunging neck lines anymore. I think there's a time when you can really look great, but you have to address it properly.
>
> (Natalie, 60, administrator)

Peer-group support was not only desired but required an identity reconstruction through attire as a gendered artefact for presentation of self at work. There was a sense that women should support each other with regard to making an effort with the presentation of bodily ageing at work. Several women suggested that an agentic approach to not only 'help ourselves', but where women should support each other: 'we appreciate each other's efforts' (Orla, 62, nursery nurse). Further, there was a sentiment that women in mid- to later life do have a responsibility to act as role models for younger 'older' women as summarised by Laura:

> I think if more women in their 60s were presented like that, it would make [ageing] more attractive, definitely . . . women can help women . . . enjoy being an older woman.

While attire had the power to act as a 'cultural mediator' shaping how experiences of ageing are 'imagined, experienced and performed at an embodied level' (Twigg, 2012), it appeared that this could also act as a cultural reinforcer when outdated images of women in mid- to later life were insufficiently replaced with modern contexts. These women actively and agentically engaged in identity work to rebuff this culturally reinforced perception of dressing an ageing body. Without a clear alternative, they appeared to be pioneers in determining how to dress their ageing bodies through the perceptions of meaningful out-group others balanced with their own aesthetic desires of what 'older' should mean.

Representing a challenge to appearing contextually appropriate, a common narrative around bodily changes due to the natural process of menopause, menopausal-related joint pain was cited as a reason that participants could no longer 'dress up', i.e. 'because now I am post-menopausal . . . I am no longer able to wear high-heeled shoes . . . the bones in my feet just won't allow me to do it' (Catherine, 51, counsellor). Similarly, Monica identified her ageing body – specifically, a 'gammy hip' – as the reason to adopt a style of clothes that did not match her colleagues who dressed in skirts and heels. Her choice was to not conform to attire norms due to discomfort felt by her ageing body, whereby dressing up might adversely impact physical health.

> I try to wear flatter shoes . . . trousers . . . jumpers and maybe more casual clothing so I think that then reflects in my working life . . . . I'm confident enough to wear what I'm comfy in. I'm on the floor with the children, so I will wear trousers. I'm not going to dress up in skirts like some of the girls. I'm in the playground; I get cold; I will wear lots of layers, so you know I'm wearing what I'm choosing to wear around my own comfort . . . . I do think that if I was to really dress up, it would affect me health-wise with my hip . . . . I also think that it makes it harder for me to do my job.

Being dressed appropriately was important for women across a range of industries and was associated with organisational and personal trust and professionalism.

> you can trust us; there's something about being able to trust someone in their sphere, correctly dressed . . . in my area, most people are suited and booted.
>
> (Rachel, 50, lawyer).

Tania, a 50-year-old academic, voiced a common theme among participants around how colleagues responded favourably to her when she changed her attire at work to what she deemed appropriate to her elevated occupational status (i.e. from senior lecturer to professor).

> I dressed smarter and that gave me more confidence and I think it probably changed the dynamics . . . to change my appearance and look more professional at work . . . with male peers . . . not consciously, just a feeling, a perception.

For Tania, changing her attire to what she perceived as more appropriate or 'smarter' was to dress herself in a more masculine manner, moving away from long flowing skirts to more tailored attire, thus confounding her 'feminine subject' (Swail & Marlow, 2018). She looked to her male colleagues for their approval, which – when given – resulted in her increased confidence at work. In the absence of an appropriate role model, Tania engaged in experimentation with how to present her ageing body at work through attire, gauging perceptions of male colleagues as a guide to her success or otherwise.

Tania's necessity for change was not felt by all participants. Problematising this general sentiment of dressing appropriately for the job, the company, the industry, several participants spoke to the theme that dressing the ageing body was more complex and effortful.

> I try and dress the part . . . as you get older you have to put more effort in . . . which makes me less confident . . . definitely there's a challenge for women of age to present themselves in a way that suggests they are still very much in touch with current thinking and trends.
>
> (Georgina, 55)

> . . . we live in an atmosphere that's very subtle . . . there is a certain pressure here to look good in your appearance, what you wear.
>
> (Laura, 50)

> . . . enough that I pass muster with the [students], but not so much that I would feel that I was pandering to them or society's ideas about how women are supposed to waste their time on trying to look a particular way . . . .
>
> (Julia, 50)

Laura referred to contextually appropriate dressing and grooming an older body as 'subtle', which highlighted the exposure for engaging in counter-productive or simply 'wrong' identity work. For these women, identity work to dress in a contextually appropriate manner led to decreased confidence (Georgina) or increased pressure (Laura), and for Julia it was about balancing what would satisfy meaningful out-groups (students, society) with her own sense of self-identity by not pandering to these out-groups. Further, that sentiment appeared contextually dependent based on the intersection of industry and occupational type. Ursula, an administrator working in an environment, which by her own admission does not place value in the appearance of attire, said:

> I know a lot of ladies my age are immaculately groomed and quaffed . . . as long as I'm clean and tidy, that's all that matters . . . . I don't think they give a toss what I wear . . . .

It was clear from participant narratives around attire that identity work was conducted to present themselves at work in the best light or to 'get it right', motivated by fear of getting it wrong. Being aware of what was deemed appropriate by a range of significant out-group members, arguably positioned by the participant as the dominant authority, was important. For some participants, their ageing bodies presented a barrier to achieving the perceived desired appearance norm. Identity work, whether through demonstration of skills or ability (exemplified here by Isla) or through hiding the ageing body presented an opportunity to compensate for perceptions of breaching contextually appropriate appearance norms:

> . . . if you're like me and 20 stone and you don't have a suit on and you're sitting next to someone who's a size 12 in a suit, [they're] going to believe that person before me . . . [but then] it's more about what your capability . . . you can demonstrate that you don't have to wear the suit to actually have something to offer.
>
> (Isla, 58, project manager)

Identity work through attire as a gendered artefact at work appeared to represent a navigation through a controlled choice. This choice, while seemingly agentic and personal, was conducted within the contextual confines of the industry, the job and even the tasks to be performed on any given day. This controlled choice was to be managed through heuristics or implied rules set by a range of stakeholders: different and same-sex peers, organisations, clients, students and perceptions of societal norms of gendered ageing bodies and seemingly predominantly younger out-group others at work. Navigating this controlled choice was assisted for participants who could draw upon adequate role models (from same-sex workers in mid- to later life, industry norms and organisational standards); however, a sense of precarity or fear of getting it wrong was experienced by participants who were exposed to choose without access to appropriately aged same-sex role models.

6.5 Chapter discussion

Working in mid- to later life was viewed as a period of transition whereby all participants in some form engaged in identity work around liminal practices and behaviours. These were largely based on perceptions of out-group others. In terms of continued labour force participation, participants generally expressed a desire to continue working, regardless of financial requirement. However, this desire to work was affected by how participants differentially approached their older worker identity whereby perceptions of self and others emerged as a source of action. Perceptions of self and others appeared to provide differing mechanisms behind how participants conducted identity work. Table 6.1 shows how these internal and external mechanisms of age-related appearance-based perceptions led to a variety of approaches to dialogic construction of identity work (Beech, 2011) and experiences of liminality (Ibarra & Obodaru, 2016). Further, the term or label 'older' provoked reactions suggesting its lack of neutrality; this chapter challenged the appropriateness of this term when describing, defining and categorising workers over 50 years of age. Chapter 7 will continue this consideration of 'older' and discuss how, through liminal practices, participants made sense of their ageing bodies at work.

Table 6.1 Chapter 6 findings

Source of action	*Perceptions of self*	*(Meta)perceptions of others*
	Personal standard and responsibility	Comparison with out-group others, lack of age-appropriate role models
Dialogic construction of identity work (Beech, 2011)	Inside-out initiation, experimenting for balance of seeking authenticity with social construction of ageing	Two-way reflection, seeking or reacting to active inclusion, foreground experience valued by others
Liminality (Ibarra & Obodaru, 2016; Turner, 1969)	Self-guided process, self-preservation	Highly institutionalised, influenced by out-group others
Themes	Stereotyped by self, presentation of ageing as 'not-old'	Connection with others, stereotyped by others, age-appropriate context

The paradoxical phase of experimentation was represented by a desire to express oneself in a flamboyant or personal way, freeing oneself of the shackles of the social construction of appearance, though mindful that this expression of identity might expose the worker to value judgements, such as being out of touch or showing poor judgement, symptomatic of age-related changes. Stereotypes are powerful in informing the expected identity of the older worker (Riach, 2007), and this fear of embodying the personification of age stereotypes was an understandable response. The emotional response of fear was reported as a reaction to identity-threatening situations (Down & Reveley, 2009), and these findings extend that view; fear also resulted from the perception of free and natural self-expression. Ibarra and Obodaru (2016), however, posit that with fear of a transitional identity comes anticipation and excitement, suggesting that fear is part of the liminal state to be navigated.

The majority of participants actively reacted to the term 'older', signifying that it is not a neutral term (Hurd Clarke & Griffin, 2008; Slevin, 2010; Thomas et al., 2014). Participants conducted identity work through the liminal transition of ageing (Beech, 2011), experienced by participants transitioning to a socially constructed identity of the 'older worker' reinforcing Alvesson et al.'s (2008, p. 15) 'identity work as a continuous process'. As highlighted by Riach (2007), I proceed with caution at accepting the truism of the term 'older worker' as simply those who have reached the somewhat arbitrary age of 50 years. Identity work was conducted to either accept or reject the older worker label; however, data revealed the influence of self and meta-perceptions as a mechanism for how participants identified with older.

Findings extend Beech's (2011) liminal identity work model. While data present a similar division to those of Beech (2011) in terms of recognition supporting a discourse of either an epiphany or the gradual dawning of entering this liminal position, the majority of participants (all but one) reported the latter. The term 'older worker' was rejected by some participants who refused this narrative as socially legitimate (Turner, 1969). Neither was there a sense of incomplete or culturally problematic narrative through this rejection (Ibarra & Obodaru, 2016), suggesting that a refusal of being labelled as 'older' meant that liminality was fleeting and inconsequential, and even potentially was not experienced through a lack of consent of the worker. Conversely, other participants felt bound to the term older worker, accepting – even embracing – its identification as socially legitimate (Turner, 1969). The individualised responses to ageing at work were not protected by or indicative of income or seniority in the world of work, revealing a homogeneity of experience within the heterogeneous 'older worker' group (Taylor et al., 2016).

A key contribution of this chapter is a nuanced understanding of how self and meta-perceptions (Meister et al., 2014) differentially influenced attitudes to work in later life. Understanding gendered identity at work was conducted and performed 'through the body' (Hurd Clarke, 2018). As with recent work on the presentation of the ageing body at work, pressures to maintain a youthful appearance created a paradox between the presentation of a natural and an unnatural body whereby an ageing body must 'continue to appear youthful well into mid-life' (Carter, 2016) and the desire to age naturally can be overshadowed by social and organisational constraints and expectations (Cameron et al., 2019). As such, an authenticity paradox (Ibarra, 2015) resulted from a desire to look natural without looking older. As with the previous chapter, 'be older, but don't look it', became a central challenge to identity and attitudes to work in response to (internalised) gendered ageism.

Through their narrative of identity, participants generally reported that it was their personal responsibility to present themselves as youthful in body, which they understood and performed in direct comparison with their own younger bodies (Moya-Garofano & Moya, 2019; Schilling, 2015) or their younger selves at work. The identity work of body work was conducted to mask the appearance of ageing on the body, which was in contradiction to a desire of a natural-looking bodily appearance. Due to its 'naturalised temporal component', ageing leads people to avoid categorisation, as opposed to gender, where group members tend to identify themselves without hesitation (Calasanti & King, 2018), through a comparison of oneself back in time (Krekula, 2016), which was reinforced through these findings whereby participants rejected categorisation as older through foregrounding their younger bodies. Accepting yet rejecting natural bodily ageing seemingly positioned participants in a liminal space of older-not-old, natural-not-natural. While identity work is generally conducted to gain plausibility and coherence (Alvesson & Wilmott, 2002; Brown, 2015; Caza et al., 2018), identity work was seemingly lacking in direction. Identity work to resolve this dissonance was conducted through 'giving in' when there was a shame in 'fighting' the natural ageing process; however, the alternative was to contravene societal expectations of the presentation of the female body, without recourse to the natural processes of ageing.

Previous studies report that dialogic construction interacts between the self and the other; however, here this is extended to the self and the perceived other. Indeed, we could take this a step further, through meta-perceptions, and suggest that this dialogic exchange is through the perceived self and the perceived other, creating a situation whereby identity work through a relational discourse was conducted upon a constructed reality of thoughts, actions, feelings and emotions. Reflective identity work practices, characterised by perceptions (Beech, 2011), were used to make sense of the perception of bodily ageing in response to how participants felt that they were viewed in the world of work.

Identity work was conducted in response to being stereotyped by others, highlighting the importance of a relational connection with generally out-group others in how identity work was conducted and how gendered ageism was internalised. These nuanced findings on the importance of perceptions of others addresses a lack of empirical studies on how work attire is experienced and used by women in mid- to later life to manage the appearance of bodily ageing at work. Drawing on seminal work conducted by Julia Twigg (2007, 2012), this chapter provides evidence of 'attire as identity work' for women in mid- to later life, a hitherto under-explored area in studies on the workplace. The controlled choice around attire (Howlett et al., 2015; Caven et al., 2013) was conducted to present the work identity in the best light (Caza et al., 2018); however, there appeared to be uncertainty around how to dress the older, ageing, changing body at work, arguably associated with a lack of appropriate role models.

Participants appeared to default to an outdated model of how older bodies were dressed at work, reminding us that individuals tend to naturally seek out (slightly) older role models (Gibson & Barron, 2003). In the absence of appropriate role models, respondents defaulted to an arguably outdated stereotype to which they were simultaneously drawn (Ibarra, 1999) but also repelled: 'I don't want to become'; 'I avoid'; 'I'm looking for something'. However, identity narrative was arguably one of uncertainty around how to act, look and/or dress. Participants appeared to acknowledge of a transitional phase of becoming older (Alvesson et al., 2008) but actively engaged in identity work to avoid perceptions associated with gendered ageing. The discourse used was relatively old-fashioned – 'frump'; 'fuddy-duddy'. By building up a potentially outdated model in their minds, these women actively worked to reject their version of an ageing identity. Identity work here was the avoidance of a seemingly outdated stereotype of what women in mid- to later life look like or what they should wear at work and walking the tightrope of acceptable sexuality versus sufficiently youthful appearance (Trethewey, 1999). This was evidenced by the discursive identity work in which participants engaged relevant to perceptions of themselves, creating a conflicted identity of transition to becoming older. Twigg (2007, 2012) posited that attire is not only an expression of identity but are objects of transition.

Extending current thinking, participants appeared to accept the transition of ageing but rejected the artefacts or objects of attire available to them to do so. For women in male sex-type jobs, there appeared to be a clear vision of what they should wear at work to reinforce their appropriate job-contextualised image, but how to wear it was a cause of concern for some women due to the changing shape of their older bodies. Here, the goal of identity work was looking the part, conforming and being aware of evolving expectations in order to gain respect, confidence and trust at work. Negotiation of identity through the transition of becoming older or being perceived as older at work was met with an exposure to the risk of unsuccessful identity work to conform. This jeopardised or precarious conformity might result in individuals being perceived to 'lose the plot' of their identity (Beech, 2011, citing Thomas & Linstead, 2002) or breach implicit or explicit group rules on what is accepted and expected as socially constructed appearance norms (Langlois et al., 2000).

Identity work as agentic behaviour (Coupland & Brown, 2012) allowing for a bodily display of taste (Cutcher & Achtel, 2017) was mobilised by perceptions of what 'older' women at work 'should' look like. Such attitudes give value and subjective power to the otherwise banal word: should. This cast doubt on just how free women in mid- to later life are to choose how they display their bodies at work. These findings speak to the transitional nature of becoming – rather than being – older (Alvesson et al., 2008; Ibarra, 1999), whereby a formally stable worker identity was disrupted, triggering feelings of uncertainty, anxiety or self-doubt. Reconciliation to this identity dissonance was sought through seeking role models, but this appeared unsuccessful for some as such respondents' identity work was conducted as mitigation, reflecting Skeggs' (1997) assertion that identity work conducted by workers in mid- to later life 'is only to stop things from becoming worse' and supporting the generalised narrative of ageing as decline (Thomas et al., 2014).

Participant narrative suggested that a connection with younger clients, colleagues and students was not only important but essential to continue (perceived) performance levels in their current job. There appeared to be a 'sweet spot' of relative age difference. However, there was an uncertainty of knowing whether the 'correct age' difference was being achieved or not, and certainly the onus was on the liminar to find this out. As such, there was the threat of not knowing when this 'right age' of relational distance might cease, leading women in mid- to later life to a precariously subjective connection with out-group members at work. This finding resonates with Duncan and Loretto's (2004) paper, which found gender and age-based discrimination resulting in workers feeling that there is never a 'right age'.

The 'right age' appeared to be found in connection with one's own perceived work identity, whereby plausibility over-rides the need for accuracy of personal narrative (Caza et al., 2018) balanced with meta-perceptions of out-group others to whom the participant wanted or even needed to relate and connect. Searching for this connection through the transition of ageing at work appeared to be relational based on age differences more so than gender, while firmly situated with experiences of (internalised) gendered ageism at work.

7 Discussion of findings – Study 1

While the ageing body was central to participants' sense of work identity (Carter, 2016; Calasanti & King, 2018), there were differences in how participants prioritised their age and gender in relation to their body and their performed identity at work. This was conducted through a work identity self-categorisation, which resonated with previous findings that identities are viewed through categorisations, such as age and gender, as those which are to be either embraced or resisted (Ybema et al., 2009). It is interesting to remember that stereotyping is activated through classification of an individual to a category (Ng & Feldman, 2012); thus, self-categorisation is important to how gendered ageism is internalised. This highlighted the nuanced and complex role of age and gender in work identity, supporting the generally accepted argument to study gender and age together as part of a whole, and to explore how different forms of inequality affect each other (Riach et al., 2015).

These identity categories were predicated by individual, organisational and contextual factors, resulting in a combination of liminal practices and dialogic construction of identity work (Beech, 2011). Alvesson et al. (2008) highlighted that identity studies have focused on 'highly localised' relational context, criticising that they often fail to take in broader contextual factors. This study supports the focus on the individualised and highly localised relational factors as being highly salient to older worker identity. While a broader context should be considered, the highly localised context should certainly not be denigrated or side-lined in favour of a broader view.

7.1 Worker: deprioritising age and gender

Participants who deprioritised age and gender, identifying simply as a 'worker', engaged in shielding identity work through positive emotive identity discourse as a result of their high confidence and authenticity of self. While recent work advocates for looking beyond the ageing body at work as gender-neutral (Taylor et al., 2016; Emslie & Hunt, 2009; Loretto & Vickerstaff, 2013), this study provides evidence that for participants high in confidence, identity authenticity and job security, a gender-neutral approach

DOI: 10.4324/9781003439257-7

to the appearance of bodily ageing was sought. This prioritised the need to be seen as a worker, not a worker who was older or was categorised through gender despite evidence that people tend to readily categorise themselves by gender but avoid doing so with age (Calasanti & King, 2018). Confidence and a strong sense of worker identity allowed for age and gender to be deprioritised in how participants entered into identity work based on how they felt that they were being perceived (meta-perceptions) at work through their performance and cultural and job fit (Carter, 2016; Sabelis & Schilling, 2013; Hurd Clarke, 2018; Calasanti & King, 2018; Trethewey, 1999). It should be stated, though, that the women who rejected both age and gender categories did not appear to suffer from gendered constraints including an 'uneven and stalled' employment trajectory constraints (Loretto & Vickerstaff, 2013; Damaske & Frech, 2016) or gender inequality in position (Bowman et al., 2016).

Despite the fact that gender was deprioritised, it is argued that normative gendered effects were not part of the worker identity; as such, their experiences of ageing might model the male experience of work more than the normative female experience. Participants in this category seemed to reject subtle discrimination and internalised ageism based on their age and/or gender. This is contra to previous findings of age and gender discrimination at work in that participants were able to thrive at work through experience and knowledge (Jyrkinen & McKie, 2012), reject age stereotypes (Jones et al., 2017; Mavin et al., 2016), and shield against unconscious bias from out-group members (Roscigno et al., 2007). While the literature on aesthetic labour suggests that perceived economic value is gendered (Foweraker & Cutcher, 2019; Warhurst & Nickson, 2007), these women – who deprioritised the importance of the body or exhibited a youthful body – embraced a gender-neutral work identity. Being seen as a worker and not an older and/or female worker was a benefit; however, unlike studies which suggest that this requires a masculinisation of the female body (Swail & Marlow, 2018) or sexlessness (Twigg, 2012) or gender-neutrality (Trethewey, 1999), it is simply that an age and gender dialogue was deprioritised below the importance of the ability to perform at work, and pursuing value in the workplace.

While general physical health is the most commonly cited barrier to extending working lives in Europe (Edge et al., 2017), participants who viewed themselves as simply 'workers' did not engage in a dialogue around performative decline (Riach, 2007) or adverse health associated with ageing. The appearance of positive health was indeed associated with a youthful appearance (Hurd Clarke & Griffin, 2008; Slevin, 2010; Thomas et al., 2014; Carter, 2016; Cameron et al., 2019). The social construction of how we are told, explicitly or implicitly, that we should look at a given age and stage of life (Hurd Clarke, 2010, 2018) was not ignored. It was internalised by those who spoke about their appearance as either youthful or unchanged; as such, there was little or no threat to work identity (Petriglieri, 2011) and therefore required no solution (Clarke et al., 2009; Alvesson et al., 2008). Participants who deprioritised both gender and age engaged in identity work to present themselves through an authentic sense of having something to offer society (Riach & Loretto, 2009) and/or embodying the 'ideal worker' as someone who has not actually aged at all (Carter, 2016; Rowe & Kahn, 2015, 1997). Successful ageing for these workers equated to a power to deprioritise age and gender and to control the impact of perceptions of others through identity work based on authenticity and confidence (Goretzki & Messner, 2019; Meister et al., 2014).

While theory suggests that identity work is at its most active and intense when under threat or conflict (Caza et al., 2018; Beech, 2011), identity work was conducted by workers despite the absence of identity threat or conflict. Dialogic construction of liminal identity was inside-out (Beech, 2011), with little or no impact of reflected appraisal (McMullin & Cairney, 2004) or meta-perceptions (Carlson et al., 2011). Workers were not seeking an idealised self or 'optimal distinctiveness' (Beech, 2008; Brewer, 1991); they were simply following their established career trajectory. There was a sense of liminality that followed Turner's (1969) classic conceptualisation rather than modern extensions (Ibarra & Obodaru, 2016) whereby the liminar followed a socially legitimate path guided by visible and appropriate role models (Gibson & Barron, 2003; Ibarra, 1999). This was evidenced through an unchallenged acceptance of chronological age and being older. Further, shielding behaviours could potentially extend the protective barrier to ageing at work, creating a self-fulling virtuous cycle of confidence in perceptions around the appearance of bodily ageing.

7.1.1 Identifying as an older worker and/or a gendered older worker

The majority of participants did identify as older, understanding that their chronological age equated to not only a transitional phase of work identity but a sense of becoming older, or at least perceived as older but not necessarily associating with that age categorisation: 'betwixt and between'. The chronological age of 50 years was an important marker of chronological age for participants in the transition of older, suggesting that calls for its subordination to subjective age (Kotter-Grühn et al., 2016) be taken with caution. However, findings support that chronological age is no longer a 'unique reference point of the truth of ageing' (Tulle & Krekula, 2013), as participants differentially either accepted or rejected chronological age and the older worker label. As such, inclusion of both chronological and subjective age(s) should not be discounted in future research on ageing.

Ageing, for some participants, presented an opportunity to engage in identity work to reinvent and reposition themselves at work. However, this opportunity was limited in scope, as it was conducted through the ageing body, and as such was limited to an ageing aesthetic (Nickson, 2018; Warhurst & Nickson, 2009). This was exemplified by the type of identity work conducted, which was to prioritise a personal narrative and relational dialogue around experience and wisdom to create a sense of value and importance whereby an ageing appearance might otherwise threaten the perceived value of work identity. Ibarra (2015) found that managers believed that they should self-promote their experience to establish value at work, which is supported and extended by this finding of foregrounding the maternal body at work as identity work. In line with previous work on identity adaption (Ibarra, 1999; Alvesson et al., 2008), participants identifying as older – but not necessarily as older women – used an inside-out dialogic construction of experimentation as a liminal practice, which was not found in the original liminal identity work application (Beech, 2011). Identity adaption requires internal/external evaluation, which was conducted through experimental liminal practices by participants (Beech, 2011). However, it is crucial to note that these practices were conducted largely through perceptions of out-group others to capitalise on looking older, addressing the call for more nuanced knowledge on how identity work is conducted (Brown, 2015). Expanding Beech's (2011) liminal identity work model, there was a sense of resolution in this behaviour: an experimental work identity given approval by out-group others was subsequently adopted as a new work identity, through the ageing body, through which value was understood and attributed.

Healthy ageing was a narrative engaged by all participants in this study. While chronological age was acknowledged, the ageing body was not as readily accepted. Identity work was conducted by women to maintain health, fitness and energy, attempting to control the inevitable ageing of the gendered body through combination of healthy, active, harmonious and productive ageing (Carpentieri et al., 2016) and through the association of positive health behaviours and youthful appearance (Carter, 2016; Cameron et al., 2019). It should be noted that a participant narrative of keeping and staying fit and healthy assumes that participants were generally fit and well, showing the relatively privileged position of these participants.

A number of participants engaged in a highly emotive dialogue around their ageing bodies, referring to their gendered ageing bodies as a threat to a separation of self, which could result in becoming invisible at work (Calasanti, 2005; Calasanti & Slevin, 2001); this was expressed by participants who experienced lowered, threatened or interrupted confidence at work. Participants who identified – willingly or not – with both age and gender engaged in somewhat chaotic liminal practices drawing on a dialogic construction of recognition of external sources. Individuals inherently work towards resolving dissonance (Petriglieri, 2011; McMullin & Cairney, 2004; Gray & Kish-Gephart, 2013; Alvesson et al., 2008), but many participants engaged in an active and performative separation of self, based on perceptions around the appearance of health and its perceived value within the world of work. The gendered ageing body was dominated by the emotive and self-deprecating identity work on the impact of menopause symptoms (see Steffan, 2021; drawing on data from this study).

7.2 Subjective value of the older worker through perceptions of others

While it is generally accepted by identity scholars that identity work is relational (see Caza et al., 2018 for review), there remains a lack of empirical studies on the specific role meaningful others play in how individuals perform identity work – in particular, the influence wielded by or indeed relinquished to out-group others. This study found that reflected appraisal (McMullin & Cairney, 2004) and meta-perceptions (Meister et al., 2017; Carlson et al., 2011) were integral to how identity work was conducted by participants, presenting an extension to current theorising of liminality and successful ageing (Beech, 2011; Brown, 2015; Ibarra & Obodaru, 2016). Identity theory does have a rich seam of work of relational influences (Alvesson et al., 2008; Ibarra & Barbulescu, 2010), but the role of perceptions of out-group others remains unclear in identity work behaviours engaged to navigate liminal identities.

Findings in this study agree with existing thinking that identity work is conducted to portray identity as positive in relation to what is appropriate, desirable or valued within the world of work (Alvesson & Wilmott, 2002; Schein, 1975), and to emphasise distinction or the favourable aspects of worker identity (Sveningsson & Alvesson, 2003). Further, findings generally align with Ibarra's (2015) workers who sought to 'sell themselves' to promote value through experience whereby workers must 'always be on' and attuned to the social construction of how labour is valued at work and portraying themselves as actively ageing to demonstrate their value at work (Riach & Loretto, 2009), but with a twist. Identity work was conducted to seek confirmation of one's value at work through the eyes of others. The evidentiary bases of these perceptions were tenuous and, in some cases, identity work was conducted despite evidence to the contrary. Where appropriate discourses were lacking or not obvious to the participant, identity was imposed upon them through external discourses (Beech, 2011). The problem here is that available external discourses did not often match in age and/or gender appearance expectations or a lack of appropriate role models, thereby exacerbating the experience of liminality.

Findings also go some way towards answering Brown's (2015) call to address the nuances in why identity work is conducted. Participants engaged in dialogue around how they perceived they were being viewed by others, predominately younger others at work, acting as a motivator to engage in identity work. Identity work appeared to be motivated by the perception of the ideal worker (Zacher, 2015; Rowe & Kahn, 2015; Freund, 2006) as a productive body (Carpentieri et al., 2016; Langlois et al., 2000; Warhurst et al., 2009), a youthful body (Cameron et al., 2019; Carter, 2016) able to compete for resources in what is often presented as a zero-sum game (Strawbridge et al., 2002) despite the appearance of bodily ageing. Identity work was conducted to seek subjective value at work, overcoming perceptions of 'labouring bodies', whereby the gendered body is a 'problematic object', assumptions around later-life health (Edge et al., 2017; Krekula, 2016, p. 63), all of which were based on judgements of a gendered, ageing body, which for many was 'betwixt and between': older-not-old.

If the ultimate aim of identity work is a coherent identity of self and in relation to others (Caza et al., 2018), then successful identity work conducted by participants achieved a sense of plausible and coherent identity and generally resulted in positive emotional engagement with the ageing body. Confidence was identified as an individual difference which, as yet under-explored in relation to identity work, might influence the proactivity in and success of identity work, as well as in resisting the influence of perceptions (Caza et al., 2018; Winkler, 2018).

Participants drew upon meta-perceptions to guide their sense of self at work. Further, participants themselves activated stereotypes of workers in mid- to later life as less adaptable and less competent than younger workers (Gordon & Arvey, 2004), less productive (McMullin & Cairney, 2004) as peripheral and disposable labour (Loretto & White, 2006), thus working to internalise ageism through perceptions over ageing bodies at work. This supports previous findings that ageing anxiety not only affects one's own perceptions of ageing (Carter, 2016), but those who experienced ageing anxiety themselves were more likely to stereotype based on age (Shaw & Langman, 2017). While these arguably outdated stereotypes (Ng & Feldman, 2012) formed the basis of meta-perceptions around economic ageing, participant narrative was of themselves as a worker within their industry, without significant reference to gender suggesting that women in mid- to later life might be more susceptible to age than gender stereotypes.

Participants engaged in these behaviours with the explicit awareness that their perceptions of self and others might not be accurate; however, their construction of the meta-perception was powerful enough to affect employment outcomes and attitudes towards workplace retention and extending their working lives. Findings cast doubt on the applicability of Carlson et al.'s (2011) finding that people generally see themselves as others see them, which the authors refer to as an accurate meta-insight. This presents a problem, as self-perception is often based on social constructions available to the individual and are open to interpretation (Hurd Clarke, 2018; Calasanti & King, 2018; Tulle & Krekula, 2013; McMullin & Cairney, 2004). As such, this 360-degree awareness of self and others (Meister et al., 2017), inasmuch as it is actually possible, might be subject to misinterpretations and error of judgement.

Participants in this study – specifically, those with low or interrupted confidence and those who prioritised an ageing body – surrendered to an external influence of others based on meta-perceptions. Participants appealed to approval from their younger colleagues, students and clients as the source of their meta-perceptions. It could be argued that this was due to a lack of appropriate role models as aspirational figures (Gibson & Barron, 2003; Ibarra,

1999). Swail and Marlow (2018) warned that by straying too far from their expected gendered performances, individuals engaging in out-group identity work can damage personal legitimacy in the pursuit of organisational legitimacy, raising a challenge to Ibarra's (1999) role model being 'one homogenous package'. It is this lean towards a heterogenous role model 'package' that speaks to Gibson and Barron's (2003) findings from their quantitative study that workers in mid- to later life tend to create 'composite role models', piecing together a role model that helps them achieve their individual work goals. Women in this study did appear to create their own 'patchwork' (Sabelis & Schilling, 2013) role models; however, at the centre of these were a younger, arguably unrealistic embodiment of youthfulness equating with successful ageing at work. Identity work conducted through the lens of successful ageing as 'not-ageing' transferred power from role seniority and experience to tenets of aesthetic labour, or a 'body for others' (Riach, 2007). It is argued that the pursuit of successful ageing through meta-perceptions around the appearance of bodily ageing is potentially detrimental to attitudes around how women in mid- to later life work.

7.3 Women as an organisational asset

As discussed, the subjective value of women in mid- to later life at work was viewed through identity work of perceptions of out-group others. This led to findings around the management and presentation of the ageing/older body as a critical and crucial component of older worker identity (Carter, 2016; Calasanti & King, 2018, Bal et al., 2013; Twigg, 2012). Seeking the appearance of healthy ageing was seemingly motivated by the successful ageing mantra of personal responsibility and harnessing one's resources (Cameron et al., 2019; Zacher, 2015). As previously stated, healthy ageing was a narrative engaged by all participants in this study. Participant discourse and narrative around their ageing bodies was that of an organisational asset, one which is defined here as being visibly and explicitly fit for purpose, conforming with socially constructed appearance norms at work.

The prioritisation of the appearance of healthy ageing highlighted a potential danger or unintended consequences of a neo-liberal healthism (Carter, 2016). Healthism can also influence attitudes towards continued labour force participation; and second, due to the awareness of participants to engage in healthy ageing not only for themselves but as a cautionary tale for others, perhaps the consequences of looking unhealthy are not actually unintended but are instead uncontrollable. There were penalties for those who did not make the 'effort' to maintain a healthy appearance, reinforcing a blame culture (Emirbayer & Johnson, 2008); participants perpetuated this need to be seen to be making an effort in appearance specifically for and by same-sex peers. This was exemplified by warnings such as 'don't lose yourself' and it being 'not healthy for women to let their weight go', despite the natural biological cause of weight gain for menopause-aged women. This speaks to successful ageing or neo-liberal attitudes around appearance where the aim for women in mid- to later life is to 'prevent them from appearing as if they had let themselves go' (Calasanti & King, 2018, p. 15) and taking care of themselves throughout the successful ageing process (Truxillo et al., 2015).

Identity work was conducted beyond healthy ageing to include attire and grooming to present the ageing body to others at work, reinforcing previous work that attire presents the naked body, which is central to experiences of ageing (Hurd Clarke, 2018), as the self to the social world (Twigg, 2007). Identity work was conducted through attire as a gendered artefact to fit in, to 'pass muster' or to demonstrate being 'in touch with current thinking and trends', which attested to a broader ability to perform at work. Identity negotiation at work can be 'chaotic, sometimes contradictory collections' of self (Alvesson et al., 2008). While identity work was presented as a source of freedom (Calasanti & King, 2018), I suggest here that this freedom has its practical limits within the world of work, constrained by what is deemed or perceived as appropriate appearance for the gendered ageing body at work through the eyes of out-group others.

Women in Work in Mid-Life highlights the under-explored role of perceptions of self and others in how this sample of women in mid- to later life engaged in identity work to navigate the liminal path of older-not-old. Specifically, participants drew on perceptions of out-group others as the available external discourse (Ybema et al., 2009), which contra to findings, appear largely unsubstantiated by evidence (Meister et al., 2014; Carlson et al., 2011) and far more than is presented in the literature on 'older worker' identity. Participants engaged in identity work to present a 'labouring body' (Riach et al., 2015) to overcome the 'age as decline' narrative through a presentation of the ageing body as healthy (Edge et al., 2017), youthful, unchanged, consistently performative, contextually appropriate and fit for service. In short, participants sought to present the ageing body as an organisational asset, such that successful ageing at work was the ability to perform at work with a body maintained and presented by the worker. Age bias was more impactful than gender bias: internalised ageism was internalised through perceptions of out-group others, whether factual or erroneous. Gendered ageing/ageism was highly relevant as context to how meta-perceptions were understood. Identity work to overcome barriers to work were conducted through the significant influence of meta-perceptions, a hitherto under-explored area in older worker identity literature. Further, a lack of appropriate role models created an unknown and precarious path for participants whose path differed from a traditional male-normative career trajectory.

7.4 Practical and theoretical contributions – Study 1

Findings contribute to the academic literature on extending working lives and 'older worker' engagement with work and attitudes to working longer by demonstrating how women over 50 years of age engaged in identity work within the liminal space of 'becoming' older. This transitional period of bodily ageing at work is under-explored in management research and is insufficiently understood by organisational managers and HRM practitioners. Further, it is clear from these findings that looking older, feeling older and being perceived as older – rather than simply being older – reflects a period of transitional self and work identity, which is highly influenced by external discourses around ageing and older at work, leading to an internalised view of self. This study identified that female workers older than 50 engaged in identity work to maintain or reconstruct their work identities to self-promote as healthily ageing or searching for external validation of being perceived as economically ageing or being valued at work. Beyond gender, a range of individual factors affected the agency required to engage in identity work and liminal practices, all of which should be considered by future studies in this area as well as anyone managing workers in mid- to later life.

This section provides more specific detail on three key contributions from this study, discussing their potential impact on the academic conversation around extending working lives and implications for industry application of HRM of managing workers in mid- to later life. These contributions focus on highlighting the contradictions of the potentially detrimental – yet motivational – concept of successful ageing and its impact on the presentation of an ageing and potentially changing work identity as an organisational asset, and expanding existing work on liminality and identity work by demonstrating how practices are conducted by this sample of women through perceptions of gendered ageing at work.

Findings here suggest that participants conducted identity work through the ageing body as an organisational asset, whereby individual resources were called upon to present the ageing body as youthful – an image of the ideal older worker as someone who has not actually aged at all (Rowe & Kahn, 1997; Carter, 2016). Engaging in identity work around the ageing body through self-perception of healthy ageing and meta-perceptions of economic ageing was conducted by the worker for the benefit of the worker and the organisation. The contribution to what we know about workers in mid- to later life is this: there was a clear message from participants that, through the neo-liberal narrative of successful ageing (Zacher, 2015), they did not expect any investment into the maintenance of their ageing bodies from their employer. The practical implication for HRM professionals is that this does not necessarily mean that workers in mid- to later life do not want assistance and would not benefit from assistance; it simply means that there was no expectation, instead falling back on personal work ethic to engage in management and presentation of the ageing body. This suggests that an offer and acceptance mechanism of workplace support from HRM to workers in mid- to later life might be more appropriate rather than expecting workers in mid- to later life to ask for assistance in relation to their bodies.

This study presents evidence that the notion of successful ageing, a concept ubiquitously adopted and rarely challenged in management literature

(Carpentieri et al., 2017), acted as a key motivator for identity work to present the ageing body as healthy and productive. This focus on successful ageing was called into question by only one participant with her question of 'who are we successfully ageing for, anyway?'. I argue here that successful ageing, as a key motivator of identity work, raises concerns for the older worker as the comparative nature of successful ageing is more complicated: attainment of goals are measured against 'diverse standards and norms' (Baltes & Carstensen, 1996), creating an environment for 'winners and losers' (Strawbridge et al., 2002) and benefitting the resource-rich over the life span rather than the direct result of adaptive behaviours (Zacher, 2015; Freund, 2006). As yet, it appears that being perceived to be successfully ageing – be it through health or economic productivity – is what drives many workers in mid- to later life to engage in potentially harmful and self-deprecating identity work. The impact of this contribution puts the onus on HRM departments within organisations, who should explore and implement mechanisms to better support their workers in this stage of life. As organisations benefit from the maintenance of this organisational asset, so they should invest in anticipated and identified costs around retention of women in mid- to later life.

This study contributes to two key theoretical frameworks: liminality and liminal identity work. First, findings provide an extension of the Beech (2011) model of liminal identity work by demonstrating how identity work conducted by women in this study did not conform to the dialogical construction and liminal practices of the model. Further, findings suggest the importance of resolution, which is under-emphasised in the existing model – this is done by presenting identity work through liminal practices rather than liminal identity work. Second, findings provide a different view of liminality from Turner's (1969) classic conceptualisation and Ibarra and Obodaru's (2016) present-day extensions of liminality, suggesting that women in mid- to later life might present a more nuanced approach to liminality. These two contributions are discussed further in what follows.

Identity work was conducted by participants in this study to understand, manage, present, shield and hide an ageing body at work, all of which were impactful to work identity and engagement with the world of work. Findings of discursive identity work on the ageing body provided a nuanced view of how participants internalised ageist assumptions through not only self-perceptions but perceptions of others (meta-perceptions). This study contributes new and interesting findings in how meta-perceptions have influence over how and why identity work was conducted, which is a hitherto under-explored aspect of work identity construction, management and presentation.

The contribution of this study to Beech's (2011) model is two-fold. First, Beech's model touches on perceptions, but not meta-perceptions, presenting an opportunity for findings to extend this influential liminal identity work model to consider how liminal practices were used by women in mid- to later life at work. Second, this study drew on liminal identity work due to the transitional nature of ageing bodies, a hitherto under-explored area by this model. This investigation presented a different approach to liminal identity work than presented in the original model (Figure 7.1). Perceptions of self around the ageing body encouraged workers in mid- to later life to engage in liminal practices of recognition through an inside-out dialogical construction, as opposed to the original relationship with an outside-in dialogical construction; hence, the adoption of identity work.

Further, identity work was conducted where the locus of change or transition was the individual, as opposed to an organisational factor, as was the case in Beech's (2011) case studies. The impetus of transition in this book was the ageing body, not necessarily the individual's job. This implication for research suggests a new way of drawing on liminal identity work, or indeed identity work around liminal practices, to frame the relationship between women in mid- to later life and their organisations during the transition of 'becoming' older. The implication for HRM practitioners and managers suggests that older worker experiences of work – due to the perceptions around their ageing bodies more than actual physical decline – are different from other age groups and should be supported to avoid internalised ageism.

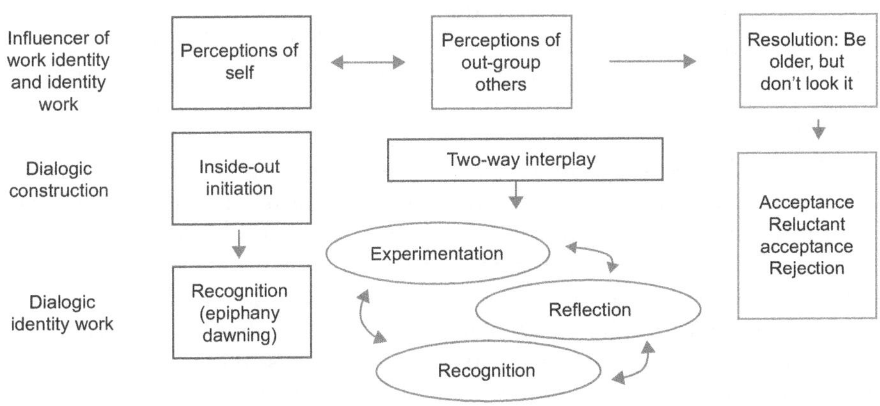

Resolution of liminality was sought through liminal identity work practices: *Be older, but don't look it.*

Self-perception of ageing (inside-out dialogue): shielding from internalised ageism, presenting the ageing body as healthy ageing, conditional acceptance of looking older. Recognition.

Meta-perceptions of ageing (two-way interplay of dialogue): capitalising on an ageing aesthetic, acknowledging value through economic ageing, negative self-affirmation of the menopausal body, relational age-stereotyping through out-group others, 'dress your age'. Experimentation, reflection and recognition.

Figure 7.1 Drawing on and inspired by Beech's (2011, p. 290) liminal identity work model, this adapted and updated model reflects ageing experiences of women in mid- to later life

Further, there is an argument to use the evidence provided here as a basis for managers to be aware of perceptions of inter-generational age bias and its impact on the whole workforce.

Perceptions of out-group others were dominated by a two-way interplay and were expressed through liminal practices of experimentation, reflection and recognition, often simultaneously. This is not to challenge the original development or application of the model; it is simply to provide evidence that application of the liminal identity work model from this sample of workers varied from its previous adoption with other age groups. The impact of this contribution is to suggest that not only do meta-perceptions have a more significant impact on identity work than previously reported (Meister et al., 2014, 2017), but that identity work conducted through the liminal space of becoming older was more chaotic than this model would otherwise allow. Further, while Beech's (2011) original paper did not allow for a sense of resolution in his case studies, there was a strong sense of the desire for resolution through liminal identity work from participants in this study, which resonated with the desire to present a plausible and coherent older worker identity (Caza et al., 2018; Brown, 2015). The difference here was that this resolution towards identity coherence was conducted somewhat reluctantly by the majority of participants due to the resistance to appearing old than was contextually desirable. Further, a general lack of role models (Ibarra, 1999; Gibson & Barron, 2003) and awareness of social normative expectations and perceptions (Cameron et al., 2019; Hurd Clarke, 2018; Caza et al., 2018; Warhurst et al., 2009) further complicated the path towards identity coherence and plausibility and ultimately resolution of older worker liminality.

This study also contributes to an understanding of liminality, which has been widely adopted in organisational literature to describe a period of transition – 'betwixt and between', which generally has negative associations (Beech, 2011; see Ibarra & Obodaru, 2016 for review of use in inter-disciplinary research). Table 7.1 represents how participants engaged with liminality through bodily ageing at work contributing a hybrid understanding of liminality between Turner's (1969) classic conceptualisation of liminality and Ibarra and Obodaru's (2016) present-day extension of liminality. This contribution addresses a previously highlighted lack of maturity in conceptual development of liminality as a framework to explore organisational aspects of transitional identities (Ibarra & Obodaru, 2016).

Findings here support Ashforth and Schinoff's (2016) suggestion that liminality is experienced when one does not possess a viable identity for the target context. Further, as 'stereotypes flourish in ambiguous performance settings' (Heilman, 1997) and 'in between' states are created in how to present bodies as revealing/hiding (Trethewey, 1999), participants in this study did appear to seek a path through the liminal space of bodily ageing as an uncomfortable state of ambiguity that was not desired for most of the participants. The contribution here is that participants were often reluctant to become the liminar,

Table 7.1 Liminality of women in mid- to later life at work, extending theories of Turner (1969) and Ibarra and Obodaru (2016)

Classic conceptualisation of liminality (Turner, 1969)	*Present-day extensions of liminality (Ibarra & Obodaru, 2016)*	*Liminality of women in mid- to later life, experiencing ageing at work*
Simultaneous role and identity suspension	Uncoupled or sequential role and identity suspension	Questioning and potential divergence of role and identity suspension through exploration
Finite, bracketed time period	Open-ended, extended time period	Highly variable time period, which might be bracketed or extended, finite or open-ended
Highly institutionalised ritual guided by elders; a built-in community of fellow liminars	Self-guided process, self-made community	Highly institutionalised ritual guided by elders for those on a traditional career trajectory; otherwise, a self-guided process due to lack of adequate role models
Socially legitimate narrative	Incomplete and/ or culturally problematic narrative; emergence of new scripts	Socially constructed narrative of ageing legitimate for those on a traditional career trajectory; otherwise, discordant with experience of ageing
Obligatory nature: the liminar has no choice but to undergo liminality	Voluntary nature: the liminar can choose to initiate liminality	Contingent controlled nature: the liminar will obligatorily age and yet variably has some form of control and choice over the appearance of ageing
Outcome is always certain. Only one possible outcome. Person assumes the next status in the 'natural order'	Outcome can be uncertain. Multiple outcomes possible. Progressive change, regressive change or unresolved status	Outcome is certain in terms of chronological ageing, yet variable ageing outcomes possible; assumption of next status in 'natural order': work until retire or resolved role and identity change or ongoing liminality of 'old-not-old'

and yet ultimately had to accept chronological ageing and succumb to a liminal position. Identity work was then conducted to make sense of the liminal path, and as stated earlier, this was specifically challenging due to the perceived lack of adequate and appropriate role models. The impact of this contribution is that, for women in mid- to later life, ageing can represent a liminal state; however, this can vary with individual differences, including confidence and emotional response to bodily ageing. HRM practitioners and managers should consider these findings as a liminar and should consider the differential level of acceptance and rejection of being labelled as an older worker in terms of the language used to manage and support an ageing workforce.

8 Study 2

Understanding value as fairness

8.1 Rationale – Study 2

Study 2 was designed to better understand the key finding of 'value' from Study 1 through a broader survey of 511 working women over 40 throughout the UK, working in a broad range of jobs and sectors. While Study 2 was a survey, there were many open text options, which provided a rich dataset from which to analyse patterns around how women over 40 work. A key finding from Study 1 was the perceived value that women placed on themselves at work, and how this was driven through comparison with others – specifically, out-group others. Participants engaged in identity work to maintain or reconstruct their work identities to self-promote as healthily ageing or searching for external validation of being perceived as economically active or being valued at work.

Engaging in identity work around the ageing body through self-perception of healthy ageing and meta-perceptions of economic ageing was conducted by the worker for the benefit of the worker and the organisation. Study 1 participants did not expect any investment into the maintenance of their ageing bodies from their employer, which I introduce here as an asymmetrical value proposition. Findings from Study 1 did not suggest that women in mid- to later life do not want assistance and would not benefit from assistance, but simply that there was no expectation from their employer, instead falling back on personal work ethic to engage in management and presentation of the ageing body. Study 1 did not seek to measure this value, in that it was discussed by participants in a subjective way, but was core to the issue of workplace engagement at their age and stage of life.

Participants from Study 1 appeared to position themselves in subordinate positions to out-group others, which is a relational experience. This is not to say that this subordination was a conscious choice; it was through a complex action of a range of factors including: internalised gendered ageism, societal expectations of being an 'older' woman and organisational culture around older/women at work. The outcome of this complex web of structural barriers and individual reactions and behaviours is that women engaged in decision-making that might have been counter-productive for themselves. As

DOI: 10.4324/9781003439257-8

such, it is important to understand broader structural barriers and influences of how women in mid- to later life work and feel valued.

Study 1 identified that women spoke about their bodies through the language of value to their organisation. Much of their experience was due to the relationship with being a women and being of a transitional, liminal age: older/not-old. While participant experience was rooted in the intersectional experience of gendered ageing (and associated gendered ageism, much of which was internalised), it was surprising that very little participant narrative was about themselves, as women, in relation to men. This is not to say that gender, gendered ageing and gendered ageism are not critical to experience of women at work, but this finding is important – that we look beyond gender so that we do not risk placing all of the emphasis of women's experiences as being in relation to those of men.

Participants spoke about their work identities in relation to displaying value to their organisation, and to meaningful (out-group) others within their world of work. For some, this was reinforcing their value; for others, this meant repositioning their value of performance at work. As such, Study 2 sought to better understand how women in mid- to later life understand their value at work, in their own right as workers and not as women-in-relation-to-men.

Study 2 was designed to explore the role of gender in how value was perceived more explicitly. To summarise, Study 2 sought to better understand how women understand or even create perceived value at work through meta-perceptions of mainly out-group others, how they perceive being economically active and how neo-liberal attitudes of personal work ethic and personal responsibilities surrounding an asymmetrical value proposition are expressed. To that end, Study 2 sought to understand *the relational experience* of women in mid- to later life, beyond the heterogeneity of the majority of approaches to manage and make policy around women in mid- to later life. Or simply put, what women found unfair about how they work.

8.2 Value Women: fair pay

We hear so much about the gender gaps, but I had a sense from conducting the interviews in Study 1 that there was another 'gap' influencing how women in mid- to later work. Women spoke about how their current work was not meeting specific personal, health, social and/or family needs, without articulating changes required to reconcile this experiential gap. Women also spoke about factors that might have to change in the future, but this was unclear in Study 1, as that line of questioning was not within the scope of the research aim. However, there was enough narrative there to motivate more direct questioning on this as part of Study 2. I was particularly interested in how women were talking about their pay. This section delves more deeply into this specific point.

8.3 Method – Study 2

During the time frame of Study 1 and developing Study 2, I conducted other research into women's health, specifically menopause. Through these other studies and the writing, lecturing and speaking engagements that I had around menopause in the workplace, I decided to open up the age profile of participants in Study 2. Study 1 was designed to capture experiences of workers over 50 in line with policy discussions at macro (government) and meso (organisational) levels. While that was appropriate for that line of questioning, I found that many of the factors that influence how Study 1 participants interacted with their world of work preceded 50. As such, I made the decision to survey and interview women over 40 for Study 2.

I conducted a survey using the Prolific recruitment platform on 'How women in mid- to later life work', which included questions around health and well-being at work, psychological capital, burnout, workplace engagement and performance, and how much unpaid care is performed while engaging in paid work. I also asked a range of open text questions around work 'gaps', motivated by those that I outlined in the introduction (Section 1.2) of this book. Specifically, these questions were designed to elicit a response to any factors that contribute positively and negatively to engaging in paid work now and in the future.

The criteria for survey inclusion was simply for the participant to identify as a woman, be in paid employment, and be over 40 years of age. The survey was completed by 511 women working in the UK in a range of industries and job types, who provided survey responses (quantitative data) and also the majority open text responses (qualitative data).

8.4 Findings – Study 2: fairness pay gap

I present findings into how participants reported their pay as being 'fair' or not. First, the reality of fair pay for women in this study was complex, with a range of factors at play to determine fairness of pay. What was surprising was that comparison of gender (or the gender pay gap) was far from the determining factor of fair pay for women. Of the 511 overall survey respondents, 502 women gave a viable response to this question: 'Do you think your pay is fair for the work that you do?' Of these 502 respondents, 320 (63.7%) reported that they work full-time.

Much has been written about the gender pay gap, which is the value and fairness of women's pay in relation to men's pay. While this broader research is crucial, what is often missed is a 'fairness pay gap'. Women's workplace experience, rights and adjustments have been discussed and measured in relation to the experience of man as the model worker; however, the approach taken in *Women in Work in Mid-Life* is to focus on women in their own right, not as positioned in relation to men.

Fairness was more about fair pay for the job itself, and less about gender comparisons. While study and awareness of gender pay gaps is crucial, Study 2 set out to explore fair pay as about the job itself rather than as a comparison of women against men. For women who worked part-time (36.3% of total sample), fairness appeared to be more about the job, and less focused on gender differences (i.e. pay gap). In the part-time group of respondents, there was not a single example in the open text comments relating to gender comparison, suggesting that women's pay should be measured in relation to what is fair, based on the job and the range of factors previously suggested. The danger of focusing on the gender pay gap is that men in a range of underpaid jobs might also be poorly paid. If a company should only be required to report on their gender pay gap, there is a risk that widespread underpayment of all workers will go under-reported. Full-time workers (63.7% of the total sample of Study 2) were more likely to refer to gender pay differences as a reason for unfair pay. This could be because women working full-time are more likely to compare with male full-time workers and because women are more likely to work part-time than men, reducing the basis of comparison.

In response to the survey question: 'Do you think your pay is fair for the work that you do?', 39% of the 502 respondents replied 'yes'; 37% replied 'no', 21% said 'maybe' and 3% chose not to disclose their pay or whether they felt it was fair. For this analysis, due to space constraints, I have presented full-time employees (or workers if self-employed) as the percentages are representative of those of the whole sample of responses. I was interested in the categories of responses, i.e. 'yes', 'no' and 'maybe', which are reported in more detail in the section that follows.

8.4.1 Factors influencing fair pay

Regardless of the amount of pay, respondents were more likely to report 'yes' that their pay was fair when their pay was an appropriate fit with their job. These findings were largely consistent over a range of income brackets. There appeared to be an acceptance of earning lower pay when the job had lower stress and responsibility. Most of these factors can be described as within-job factors unique to the individual, while the theme of comparison was generally external to the individual and their job.

Note that the following quotes and subsequent analysis are from women earning less than £2,000 per month gross salary (or income if they are self-employed) for full-time work. The average UK monthly gross salary for women is £2,937, so the women in this category are paid below the average. Incidentally, the average monthly salary for men in the UK is £3,521 (Statista, 2023).

Of the 502 respondents in total and 320 who work full-time, 99 respondents reported earning less than £2,000 per month gross salary. Of these 99 respondents, the majority (51%) reported that they felt their pay was unfair.

It was not surprising that this was a majority, but I did expect the percentage to be much higher. Respondents who felt that their pay is fair was 21%. While this is a lower percentage, it is arguably still high, as their pay is lower than average in the UK. However, as this analysis suggests, feelings of fair pay are far more complicated than comparison with one metric, such as reporting of gender gaps or comparison of average pay. I was also interested in reasons behind a 'maybe' response (26%) as to why there is uncertainty around the fairness of pay for those earning less than the average pay for women in the UK.

Even among women who recognised their relatively low pay (i.e. below the UK average), they did not necessarily deem it unfair due to the trade-off against and between work-related factors, which taken together created a greater sense of ease, including: responsibility, autonomy and flexibility. These factors were also inter-related with the umbrella theme of comparison as a basis for fair pay. There were many different comparators that were relevant to a fair pay calculation by respondents. The following quotes exemplify these findings in more detail.

Respondents discussed a trade-off between pay and factors of ease, including an easy commute, low responsibility and a sense of fairness. The following quotes cite the respondent age, job type, and hours worked (rather than contracted) per week.

> I am happy with the amount of pay I receive, and I can cycle to my work place, which reduces any added travelling costs.
>
> (52, Social Care, 30 h/w)

> It is administrative and not strategic. I have little responsibility.
>
> (47, Administration in Civil Service, 37 h/w)

> I receive decent pay for what I do.
>
> (47, Self-employed in Research, 50 h/w)

The level of autonomy that is experienced at work was a common theme among women who answered yes to being paid fairly. For example:

> I think I'm paid well for the hours I work because I'm my own boss so no one takes part of my payment from me.
>
> (54, Health & Social Care, 30 h/w)

Comparison with others was an interesting theme as there were a range of 'others' that were used as a basis of comparison of pay to deem it fair or unfair including: colleagues, managers, other companies, other industries, previous pay, pay not keeping up with inflation and even comparison with their teenage children. For example:

> . . . it is more than the zero hours pittance I earned before at a university.
>
> (51, Professional in Education, 30 h/w)

> I am paid an hourly rate that is paid to everyone in my position.
>
> (57, Teacher, 30 h/w)

> It is a higher rate than in the private sector.
>
> (55, Administration and clerical in Health & Social Care, 30 h/w)

> Others have more stressful jobs but are paid less (e.g. carers on minimum wage)
>
> (44, Management in Civil Service, 40 h/w)

A common response from women indicating 'yes' to this question was to benchmark their pay against the recommended living wage; however, in the current economic crisis, it is well documented that the living wage might be insufficient for basic costs of living (UK Parliament, 2024). The 'maybe' responses followed a similar pattern of themes, although for slightly different reasons. Comparison with others included reasons such as transparency around gender pay equality, to a lack of knowledge of how much others earn, so it was unclear where a 'maybe' response was driven by how informed a respondent was about pay. For example:

> I have not done enough research on pay and not sure of wages of others and the going rate.
>
> (52, Health and Social Care, 35 h/w)

Gender was only an issue for full-time workers. As previously stated, surprisingly, part-time workers did not mention gender pay differences or comparisons at all. It seemed that acknowledging no gender difference through transparency was not enough to move away from ambiguity over whether pay is fair.

> We are all on the same differing pay scales regardless of sex.
>
> (61, Call Centre in Accountancy, Law, Finance, 35 h/w)

It was common that the 'maybe' response came from a sense that the pay did not fit the job that was done, as well as a comparison with the pay of others in a similar grade. For example:

> I feel like my role should be regraded in line with the duties I do – I feel there are others who do similar work but are on a higher grade.
>
> (45, Administration in Teaching, 30 h/w)

Many responses were relevant to industry norms and expectations, unsure of how skills and experience translated to other contexts of work.

> I could probably charge more for the level of knowledge, skills and experience I have. I work in a profession where there is an ex

> pectation that people will work for free or low wages even after qualification.
>
> (67, Self-employed Counsellor, 15 h/w)

Again, the trade-off between pay and flexibility and autonomy was acknowledged, but this time creating sufficient uncertainty to provide a 'maybe' response to fair pay. For example:

> Well, it's not bad considering how much holiday I get, and that I love my job!
>
> (49, Teacher, 40 h/w)

> I work from home so my pay works out OK with no commuting costs, etc.
>
> (48, Administrator in IT, 50 h/w)

Respondents who reported that their pay was not fair for the work that they do (53%) overwhelmingly reported this theme because of comparison with others, although this comparison was made against a number of factors, as exemplified by the following quotes.

Comparison with people on benefits:

> I work 5–6 hours a day and earn very little; my son is on benefits, and sometimes get more than I do for doing nothing!
>
> (52, Administrator in Business & Management, 30 h/w)

Comparison with other sectors:

> Other sectors are paid more but because I need to work term time only I have no option but to work in education.
>
> (50, Administrator in Teaching, 30 h/w)

Comparison with other business in the same sector:

> My employer generally pays employees lower than comparable businesses.
>
> (40, Software Tester in IT, 30 h/w)

Comparison with overseas workers who might be more cost-effective for the employer:

> I am competing with people in many countries [where] there is no minimum wage, no holiday pay, no sick pay.
>
> (48, Creative Arts & Media, 30 h/w)

Comparison with colleagues (where there is the perception of working hard, or not):

> I work really hard (probably one of the few staff in the company who is 'on' the entire time), and yet am one of the lowest-paid roles.
>
> (49, Administration in Accountancy, Law, Finance, 37.5 h/w)

Comparison with colleagues (where there is inadequate pay to demarcate between seniority or hierarchy):

> There is very little pay divide between me and the team I manage.
>
> (40, Management in Retail/Wholesale, 38 h/w)

Comparison with minimum wage:

> The hours I put in equate to making less than minimum wage.
>
> (40, Self-employed, Public & Civil Service)

It is curious to see here that perceptions of comparison is a driving force of felt value as with Study 1. In addition to comparison with a range of out-group others and factors, respondents who indicated that they felt overworked and undervalued was the other most significant theme of those who felt that their pay is unfair. The following quotes summarise these overlapping themes of feeling overworked and undervalued. Where the physical toll of the work on the body is not taken for consideration in the pay provided, an unfair and unbalanced value proposition at work is created.

> . . . the work is physically demanding, and it causes injuries and strain on the body.
>
> (50, Driver, 35 h/w)

> My work is tough and manual.
>
> (53, Environment & Agriculture, 40 h/w)

This value proposition was also expressed through a narrative of not being appreciated, through fair pay, for the quality of the work provided:

> I work many hours and I'm offering a great service; I would deserve much more.
>
> (53, Self-employed, Creative Arts & Media, 45 h/w)

This comment is reflective of many who work in sectors that are highly regulated yet low paid (for example, social care, health and academia). There was a strong theme that highly specialised work should receive recognition in pay. In such sectors, which employ a high proportion of women, the barriers to entry are high and yet remuneration insufficiently reflects these entry criteria and the ongoing effort of the job itself. For example:

> I work in the third sector and within social care, both of which are generally low paid. My current role pays significantly lower than previous jobs despite having higher requirements in terms of professional training.
>
> (47, Professional in Third Sector, 40 h/w)

> It requires specialist knowledge of information, data protection and social services departments, and requires minimum degree level training (which I have). I'm not the lowest paid in my organisation but I am in the lower bracket, and it took 13 years to get a pay increase that would more closely align with what I do.
>
> (40, Management, Public & Civil Service, 40 h/w)

> I get paid just above the minimum wage for a job that requires training and is quite specialised. My wages have stayed the same for the last 10 years.
>
> (55, Quality Control in IT, 40 h/w)

As mentioned, gender was only referred to by full-time workers, and even then it was a relatively minor theme compared with the reported comparison factors, resulting in feelings over being overworked and undervalued:

> I work as hard as my male colleague, have been employed for 18 years but still on minimum wage.
>
> (53, Administration in Property & Construction, 35 h/w)

> I have had to start again after taking years out to care for young children.
>
> (40, Teacher, 35 h/w)

We must remember that there will often be a range of intersecting, complex factors contributing to the question of fair pay and perceived value at work. The following is an example of a range of factors at play, again reinforcing the complexities of women's life and work, which can often include emotional labour.

8.5 Discussion and conclusions: Study 2

Seeking and attributing value to women at work is more complicated than simply metrics that compare women with men. The analysis presented in Study 2 sought to extend the findings from Study 1 that how women in mid- to later life work is part of a complex web of interweaving factors around work, home, health and financial well-being. To that end, I was interested in how women felt about the fairness of their pay, as a form of perceived valued of women working in mid- to later life. Comments provided around fairness of pay were based on consistent themes of comparison with others, job autonomy and pay reflecting effort and expertise, or not being undervalued. Interestingly, the question of fair pay was a comparison of a range of factors, including, but not dominated by gender pay equality, especially relevant to full-time workers.

It is crucial that employers and policy-makers understand how workers feel about the fairness of their pay. While awareness of gender pay gaps is important, there is more to fair pay of women than as a comparison against men. Also, the gender pay gap approach perpetuates equating women's value and worth set against that of men. As such, this study provides some insight into how women determine fair pay and their perceived value at work. Fair pay appears to be a measure of within-job factors (levels of responsibility and demands; job-related stress; job autonomy; reflective of expertise and experience) and external factors (comparison with others, of which gender is a part). I recommend that management and HRM practitioners focus on factors contributing to fair pay, as well as gender pay equality at work.

It is important that women are valued based on the work that they do, and not only in comparison with men, which appears to be the basis of the current gender pay discussion and policies. Gender pay discrimination is hugely important, but if men are also underpaid, undervalued and paid less than average pay, then a gender comparison is only one aspect of support to help women obtain value for their work. Women, and those who manage and make policy about women, should be aware of how attitudes towards the fairness of pay contributes to the asymmetrical value proposition, to bring a greater balance in how women are valued by themselves and by others – identity and (meta)-perceptions of mid-life women at work.

9 Limitations of the studies

Study 1 has a number of limitations that should be considered. First, the sample used within this study was demographically narrow and it was relatively small. Second, this study presents data from a single time point, which was the interview itself, without further data collected from participants post-interview or follow-up interviews. While each of these points are discussed further in what follows, taken together, they represent limitations of this study, which future work might address in research design of data collection, analysis and interpretation.

9.1 Sample breadth and size

Participants in this study were all white and middle-class, and the majority were heterosexual. The lack of diversity among the sample provided a relatively narrow view of how women in mid- to later life experience perceptions of bodily ageing. Further, all participants in this study identified as cis-gender, meaning this study did not address minority groups of workers in mid- to later life who identify as non-binary or non–cis-gendered individuals.

Drawing on Saunders and Townsend's (2016) paper on the ideal number of participants, I sought an aspect of saturation from participant narrative and experience. However, in qualitative research tradition, Study 1 provided a rich account of participant experience and response to the research questions. There remains a challenge to the generalisability of these findings to the broader population of women in mid- to later life in the UK and beyond, non-professional groups of workers and workers in job and industry types beyond those referenced in this study. Qualitative study generally does not claim to be generalisable, as is the case here; however, these findings contribute to an important conversation about how to support women in mid- to later life to stay at work for longer.

Workers in this study self-reported as generally fit and well, whereby 82% of participants reported a very good or excellent self-rated general health. As the workforce ages, more and more workers are likely to present with natural decline of physical health as well as 'health shocks' (Loretto & Vickerstaff,

DOI: 10.4324/9781003439257-9

2013; Brown & Vickerstaff, 2011). As such, health beyond good physical health should be incorporated in further study. The literature on identity work shows that people conduct identity work to present themselves in a positive light (Caza et al., 2018), which could have influenced the self-reported figures in this study. As such, further study could also interrogate to what extent workers in mid- to later life misrepresent or position their self-rated general health in a positive light within an interview scenario and beyond in terms of the presentation of their older worker identity.

9.2 Participant engagement – a single time point study

This research draws on interviews taken from individuals at one point in their lives. While participants were encouraged to look back by drawing on life history and experiences – and indeed, to look ahead at what they envisaged of their labour force participation – many participants mentioned that this was the first time that they had really thought about ageing in relation to their work. It would have been a natural feature of the study design to follow up with participants, even a few months later, to ascertain whether they had a different understanding of ageing after that initial conversation. Similarly, Study 2 was a survey conducted at a single time point. Future research could consider multiple time points to establish a longitudinal study to further explore identity and perceptions of how women in mid- to later life at work.

10 Further research and recommendations

10.1 A broader sample: gender and health

Proposed research question: 'How do women engage in identity work to manage health conditions at work?'

It is important that further work considers minority groups of women in mid- to later life to assess whether their experiences of ageing are understood differently than the white, middle-class, heteronormative sample upon which this study is based. Further work should also include a broader range of racial backgrounds and visible disabilities, as these aspects of the individual worker will undoubtedly affect how workers are viewed and view themselves within work. It would be an interesting question to raise as to whether the experiences highlighted in this study around self and meta-perceptions would be mirrored in the experiences of those who visibly occupy membership of minority groups.

As women are expected to stay in work longer due to the extension of the SPA (Bell & Hart, 2010), studies should take into consideration age differences between workers in their 40s, 50s, 60s and beyond into their 70s. Further work should also include women in mid- to later life who do not consider themselves fit and healthy, for whom healthy ageing is more complex than staying or keeping healthy. Health shocks were outside the scope of this book. However, it would be relevant and important to consider how women who have experienced health shocks engage in identity work and would contribute to a deficit of work in this area.

10.2 Experiences of menopause at work: a longitudinal intervention study

Proposed research question: 'How can organisations better understand how women experiencing menopause symptoms want and need to be managed at work?'

DOI: 10.4324/9781003439257-10

Despite a vibrant conversation throughout society and an increasing number of workplaces (Beck & Brewis, 2024), we need to better understand how menopause influences how women work. Experiences of menopause at work and identity work to present and control the menopausal body is an emerging literature in studies on the workplace. How individual women experience menopause at work must be better understood to create practical solutions for organisations to assist and manage their older female workers, 25% of whom are likely to experience severe symptoms likely to affect intentions around workplace retention factors (ONS, 2018). There is a clear business case for organisations to invest resources to better understand and support their workers (Brewis et al., 2017; Beck & Brewis, 2024). Further work should focus on the role of line manager, especially when this relationship is reported as sub-optimal for the worker, finding an alternative line of support for the worker experiencing menopause symptoms. There are very few intervention studies on managing the menopausal body at work (Brewis et al., 2017). An intervention study that addressed these points of action would be a step towards providing a more supportive workplace for women in mid- to later life.

10.3 Comparing perceptions with meta-perceptions

Proposed research question: 'How accurate are meta-perceptions of out-group others? – A comparison of meta-perceptions with younger worker perceptions of women in mid- to later life'.

As previously indicated, participants were interviewed at one point in time. The findings in this study around perceptions and participant identity as 'older' in relation to younger colleagues, clients and students would lend itself to a longitudinal study of several time points. Further, an intervention study would also be relevant here in terms of how workers in mid- to later life engaged in 'successful' identity work. There would be a number of approaches to a longitudinal intervention study. In addition to menopause intervention previously mentioned, it would be interesting to understand how younger colleagues perceived their menopause-aged colleagues in terms of appearance of ageing. Findings from this book suggest that meta-perceptions considerably contribute to how liminal identity work affected attitudes around working longer. Duncan et al. (2000) found that university-aged students' perceptions towards older workers were largely ambivalent, despite discriminatory attitudes that older workers were likely to experience a performative decline. Their study reported a form of age-blindness by students towards workers over 50, whereby the older worker should not be discriminated against on the basis of age and yet they should not receive any special attention. A study of this kind on perceptions of younger workers under 30 working with workers over 50 might shine a light on the self-affirmative and potentially destructive nature of internalising age bias through incorrect or exaggerated meta-perceptions of out-group others.

10.4 The body as an organisational asset: individual and organisational responsibilities

Throughout this book, it has been made clear that women in mid- to later life overwhelmingly engage in agentic behaviours to understand, manage, present, mask, change and authenticate the ageing body at work. These behaviours, tactics, attitudes and strategies were seemingly created and conducted without drawing upon organisational resources. Indeed, there appeared to be little expectation of an organisational role to address the issue of bodily ageing within a professional work setting. It should be made clear that this was not the focus of the interviews in Study 1; as such, this question was never directly asked or specifically answered, so there might be more to worker expectations of their organisation than emerged from these data. Within these findings, however, participants invested personal resources to the benefit of themselves in terms of career reinforcement and enhancement, but also to the benefit of the organisation in terms of retention. It is expensive to replace workers, especially experienced workers, as such retention is – or should be – at the forefront of HRM policy in many organisations. This would also make for a relevant intervention study starting with a 'wish list' of support expectations of women in mid- to later life, followed by a tailored intervention to support identity work currently privately conducted by workers in mid- to later life themselves, finishing with a measurable outcome once the organisation has adopted and implemented key points from the older worker support wish-list. It was the question from a participant in this study: 'Who are we successfully ageing for, anyway?', which could be posed as the basis for a study of this focus.

10.5 Who are the role models for women in mid- to later life?

This study highlighted the lack of role models for older women. Despite a broad literature on this area (Schilling, 2015), there appears to be an ongoing discussion around the difference and distinction between behavioural and cognitive approaches to effective role modelling and indeed how women in mid- to later life might seek out role models. Building on Ibarra (1999), who advocated for a move away from 'one homogenous package' whereby a worker might seek a role model from one source, Gibson and Barron's (2003) study of workers in mid- to later life suggested that composite role models might be sought to compensate for a lack of clear role models, where the ideal role model is generally slightly older than oneself. Due to the increase in state pension age (SPA) in the UK and the initiatives to extend working lives, now more than ever before, it is unlikely that women in mid- to later life will have a slightly older same-sex role model to look to for either behavioural or cognitive modelling.

It would, therefore, be interesting to conduct a mixed-methods study on how women in mid- to later life look to role models – and indeed, who those role models are. Findings in this book suggest that women in mid- to later life looked to their younger colleagues or out-group others in the absence of aspirational and relevant women in mid- to later life, instead drawing on seemingly outdated tropes of looking older. This presented a danger in drawing on meta-perceptions to internalise potentially incorrect or biased perceptions of the ability or performance of the ageing body at work.

In conclusion, there are many directions that future work could be conducted from the findings in this book to create awareness of how women in mid- to later life work. While not limited to the scope of ageing studies, the transitional nature of the appearance of gendered ageing at work makes this concept particularly salient for exploration of workers in mid- to later life. Studies could focus on any one aspect of the theoretical frameworks presented within this book. The link between the emotional response to body ageing, the motivation power of successful ageing perceptions on liminal identity, the liminal space itself as a defining differentiator of women in mid- to later life, the relational power of meta-perceptions and the notion of fairness would all make for interesting follow-up studies to the findings in this book. In valuing women, we move forward with a focus on supporting women and the complexities of mid- to later life, as women in their own right and not in comparison with others, specifically with men. It is also crucial that women value themselves within the structural barriers and organisational constraints. I hope this book contributes to a management, human resource management (HRM) and organisational environment of supporting women in mid- to later life to highlight and sustain women's value at work.

Appendices

Appendix 1

Life grid example

Age	*Education/Work*	*Family*	*Health*	*Other*
20s				
30s				
40s				
50s				
60s				

Appendix 2

Topic guide for interviews – Study 1

Research goals of the interviews

- How do workers in mid- to later life experience the appearance of bodily ageing at work?

Part A: about the participant (10 mins)

1. Welcome, introduction of researcher and overview of project:
   a. We are interested in the experience of workers in mid- to later life relating to bodily ageing at work.
2. Instructions for the interview:
   a. Collect demographic and physical data (Table B.1).
   b. Sign consent form.

Table B.1 Demographic information (descriptive data)

Age (chronological):	Job title:
Gender:	Time in current role:
Marital status:	Employment type:
Children/dependents:	Subordinates:
Height/weight	Income (personal)/(household):
Highest education level:	Job satisfaction 1(poor), 5(high):

How would you rate your health? [SRH] Likert and comment

1 (poor)	2	3	4	5 (excellent)

Part B: interview (semi-structured)

- Can you tell me about your job and what it entails on a weekly basis?
- [job type complexity/sex-type]
- Can you describe how your work has changed during your life?
- What does the term 'successful ageing' mean to you personally? How does it relate to your work?
- Is appearance important to you?
- Do you think that your appearance is important to others (at work?)
- You mentioned (*health/appearance/etc.*). Can you tell me more about that? What did you do about that? [resources/strategy/capital]

Part C: direct questioning about appearance bias

If after 40 minutes, appearance has not been mentioned (or in follow up interview)

- Do you think that health and appearance are related?
- Do you think appearance is relevant to how people see you or treat you? [perception]
- Do you think appearance plays a role in your employment? If so, how did/does that make you feel?

Part D: conclusion

- Summarise discussion.
- How did you feel about talking with me about [specific subject]?
- Would you like a follow-up interview?
- If you want to follow up, contact me by email (details on information sheet).
- If you want to withdraw from this study, your data will be removed and deleted. Are you happy for me to process your data (anonymously)?

References

Abraham, J. D., & Hansson, R. O. (1995). Successful ageing at work: An applied study of selection, optimisation and compensation through impression management. *Journal of Gerontology*, 50B(2), 94–103.

Acker, J. (1990). Hierarchies, jobs, bodies: A theory of gendered organizations. *Gender & Society*, 4(2), 139–158.

Age UK. (2018). www.ageuk.org.uk/globalassets/age-uk/documents/reports-and-publications/reports-and-briefings/active-communities/rb_sept12_a_means_to_many_ends_older_workers_experiences_of_flexible_working.pdf

Age UK. (2020). www.ageuk.org.uk/information-advice/money-legal/pensions/state-pension/changes-to-state-pension-age/#

Ahuja, S., Heizmann, H., & Clegg, S. (2019). Emotions and identity work: Emotions as discursive resources in the constitution of junior professionals' identities. *Human Relations*, 72(5), 988–1009.

Ainsworth, S. (2002). The 'feminine advantage': A discursive analysis of the invisibility of women in mid to later life workers. *Gender, Work & Organization*, 9(5), 579–601.

Altmann, R. (March 2015). *A new vision for workers in mid to later life: Retain, retrain, recruit*. Report commissioned by Department for Work and Pensions.

Alvesson, M., Ashcraft, K. L., & Thomas, R. (2008). Identity matters: Reflections on the construction of identity scholarship in organisational studies. *Organization*, 15(1), 5–28.

Alvesson, M., & Robertson, M. (2006). The best and the brightest: The construction, significance and effects of elite identities in consulting firms. *Organization*, 13(2), 195–224.

Alvesson, M., & Skoldberg, K. (2000). *Reflexive methodology: New vistas for qualitative researchers*. London: Sage.

Alvesson, M., & Wilmott, H. (2002). Identity regulation as organizational control: Producing the appropriate individual. *Journal of Management Studies*, 39, 619–644.

Amabile, T. M. (2019). Understanding retirement requires getting inside people's stories: A call for more qualitative research. *Work, Aging and Retirement*, 5(3), 207–211.

Andreoni, J., & Petrie, R. (2008). Beauty, gender and stereotypes: Evidence from laboratory experiments. *Journal of Economic Psychology*, 29, 73–93.

Anyzova, P., & Mateju, P. (2018). Beauty still matters: The role of attractiveness in labour market outcomes. *International Sociology*, 1–23.

Armenta, B. M., Stroebe, K., Schiebe, S., Postmes, T., & van Yperen, N. W. (2017). Feeling younger and identifying with older adults: Testing two routes to maintaining well-being in the face of age discrimination. *PLoS One*, 12(11), e0187805.

Ashforth, B. E., & Saks, A. M. (1995). Work-role transitions: A longitudinal examination of the Nicholson model. *Journal of Occupational and Organizational Psychology*, 68, 157–175.

Ashforth, B. E., & Schinoff, B. S. (2016). Identity under construction: How individuals come to define themselves in organizations. *Annual Review of Organizational Psychology and Organizational Behavior*, 3(1), 111–137.

Bal, P. M., Kooij, D. T. A. M., & De Jong, S. B. (2013). How do development and accommodative HRM enhance employee engagement and commitment? The role of psychological contract and SOC strategies. *Journal of Management Studies*, 50(4), 545–572.

Baltes, M. M., & Carstensen, L. L. (1996). The process of successful ageing. *Ageing & Society*, 16, 397–422.

Baltes, P. B. (1997). On the incomplete architecture of human ontogeny: Selection, optimisation and compensation as foundation of development theory. *American Psychologist*, 52(4), 366–380.

Baltes, P. B., & Baltes, M. M. (1990). Psychological perspectives on successful ageing: The model of selective optimisation and compensation. In P. B. Baltes, & M. M. Baltes (Eds.), *Successful aging: Perspectives from the behavioural sciences*, 1–34. New York: Cambridge University Press.

Baltes, P. B., Baltes, M. M., Freund, A., & Lang, F. (1999). *The measurement of Selection, Optimization, and Compensation (SOC): By self-report: Technical report.* Berlin, Germany: Max Planck Institute for Human Development.

Barclay, P. (2017). Attractiveness biases are the tip of the iceberg. *Behavioural and Brain Sciences*, 17, e21. https://doi.org/10.1017/S0140525X1600042X

Bariola, E., Jack, G., Pitts, M., Riach, K., & Sarrel, P. (2017). Employment conditions and work-related stressors are associated with menopausal symptom reporting among perimenopausal and postmenopausal women. *Menopause*, 24(3), 247–251.

Beck, V., & Brewis, J. (Eds.). (2024). *Menopause transitions and the workplace: Theorizing transitions, responsibilities and interventions.* Bristol: Bristol University Press.

Beech, N. (2008). On the nature of identity work. *Organization*, 15, 51–74.

Beech, N. (2011). Liminality and the practices of identity reconstruction. *Human Relations*, 64, 285–302.

Beech, N., Gilmore, C., Cochrane, E., & Greig, G. (2012). Identity work as a response to tensions: A re-narration in opera rehearsals. *Scandinavian Journal of Management*, 28(1), 39–47.

Beech, N., Gilmore, C., Hibbert, P., & Ybema, S. (2016). Identity-in-the-work and musicians' struggles: The production of self-questioning identity work. *Work, Employment and Society*, 30(3), 506–522.

Bell, D. N. F., & Hart, R. A. (2010). *Retire later or work harder?* Discussion series paper for Institute for the Study of Labour, Germany. Reference IZA DP No. 4720.

Berger, P., & Luckmann, T. (1991). *The social construction of reality.* London: Penguin Books.

Berney, L. R., & Blane, D. B. (1997). Collecting retrospective data: Accuracy of recall after 50 years judged against historical records. *Social Science and Medicine*, 45(10), 1519–1525.

Blaikie, N. (2018). Confounding issues related to determining sample size in qualitative research. *International Journal of Social Research Methodology*, 21(5), 635–641. https://doi.org/10.1080/13645579.2018.1454644

Blane, D. B. (1996). Collecting retrospective data: Development of a reliable method and a pilot study of its use. *Social Science & Medicine*, 42(5), 751–757.

Bohlmann, C., Rudolph, C. W., & Zacher, H. (2018). Methodological recommendations to move research on work and ageing forward. *Work, Aging and Retirement*, 4(3), 225–237.

Borland, J., & Leigh, A. (2014). Unpacking the beauty premium: What channels does it operate through, and has it changed over time? *Economic Record*, 90(288), 17–32.

Bourdieu, P. (1977). *Outline of a theory of practice*. Cambridge, NY: Cambridge University Press.

Bourdieu, P. (1984). *Distinction: A social critique of the judgement of taste*. London: Routledge.

Bourdieu, P. (1990). *In other words: Essays towards a reflexive sociology*. (M. Adamson, Trans. from French). Cambridge: Polity Press.

Bowman, D., McGann, M., Kimberley, H., & Biggs, S. (2016). 'Rusty, invisible and threatening': Ageing, capital and employability. *Work, Employment and Society*, 31(3), 465–482.

Boyle, B., & De Keere, K. (2019). Aesthetic labour, class and taste: Mobility aspirations of middle-class women working in luxury retail. *The Sociological Review*, 67(3), 1–17.

Brancu, M. (2023). *Facing gendered ageism: How to retain senior women leaders*. www.psychologytoday.com/gb/blog/a-new-look-at-womens-leadership/202301/facing-gendered-ageism-how-to-retain-senior-women

Braun, V., & Clarke, V. (2006). Using thematic analysis in psychology. *Qualitative Research in Psychology*, 3(2), 77–101.

Brewer, M. B. (1991). The social self: On being the same and different at the same time. *Personality and Social Psychology Bulletin*, 17(5), 475–482.

Brewis, J., Beck, V., Davies, A., & Matheson, J. (2017). *The effects of menopause transition on women's economic participation in the UK*. Research report, Department for Education, London.

Brown, A. D. (2001). Organization studies and identity: Towards a research agenda. *Human Relations*, 54, 113–121.

Brown, A. D. (2015). Identities and identity work in organizations. *International Journal of Management Reviews*, 17, 20–40.

Brown, A. D., & Coupland, C. (2015). Identity threats, identity work and elite professionals. *Organization Studies*, 36(10), 1315–1336.

Brown., P., & Vickerstaff, S. (2011). Health subjectivities and labour market participation: Pessimism and workers in mid to later life attitudes and narratives around retirement in the United Kingdom. *Research on Ageing*, 33(5), 529–550.

Bryman, A. (2012). *Social research methods*, 4th edition. Oxford: Oxford University Press.

Business in the Community. (April 2023). *Prioritise people: Unlock the value of a thriving workforce*. www.bitc.org.uk/report/prioritise-people-unlock-the-value-of-a-thriving-workforce/. Accessed on 15/9/23.

Butler, C. (2020). Managing the menopause through 'abjection work': When boobs can become embarrassingly useful, again. *Work, Employment and Society*, 0950017019875936.

Buunk, A. P., & Massar, P. (2014). A night on the town: When the importance of mate acquisition overrides the intrasexual competition. *Anthropological Review*, 77(3), 273–285.

Byrne. (2023). Sorry, Jeremy Hunt, we older people want to work: But bosses just don't want us to. *The Guardian*. www.theguardian.com/commentisfree/2023/feb/01/jeremy-hunt-older-people-work-bosses-just-dont-want-us-to

Calasanti, T. (2005). Ageism, gravity and gender: Experiences of ageing bodies. *Generations*, 29(3), 8–12.

Calasanti, T., & King, N. (2018). The dynamic nature of gender and ageing bodies. *Journal of Ageing Studies*, 45, 11–17.

Calasanti, T., Pietila, I., Ojala, H., & King, N. (2013). Men, bodily control and health behaviours: The importance of age. *Health Psychology*, 32(1), 15–23.

Calasanti, T., & Slevin, K. F. (2001). *Gender, social inequalities, and aging*. Walnut Creek, CA: Altamira Press.
Cameron, E., Ward, P., Mandville-Anstey, S. Z., & Coombs, A. (2019). The female ageing body: A systematic review of female perspectives on ageing, health and body image. *Journal of Women & Ageing*, 31(1), 3–17.
Carers UK. (2022). *State of caring 2022 report*. www.carersuk.org/policy-and-research/state-of-caring-survey/
Carlson, E. N., Vazire, S., & Furr, R. M. (2011). Meta-insight: Do people really know how others see them? *Journal of Personality and Social Psychology*, 101(4), 831–846.
Carpentieri, J. D., & Elliott, J. (2014). Understanding healthy aging using a qualitative approach: The value of narratives and individual biographies. In D. Kuh, R. Cooper, R. Hardy, M. Richards, & Y. Ben-Shlomo (Eds.), *A life course approach to healthy ageing*, 118–129. Oxford, UK: Oxford University Press.
Carpentieri, J. D., Elliott, J., Brett, C. E., & Deary, I. J. (2016). Adding narratives to numbers in a mixed method study of successful ageing: The 6-day sample of scottish mental health survey 1947. *Sociological Research Online*, 21(2), 1–26.
Carpentieri, J. D., Elliott, J., Brett, C. E., & Deary, I. J. (2017). Adapting to aging: Older people talk about their use of selection, optimization, and compensation to maximize well-being in the context of physical decline. *Journals of Gerontology: Social Sciences*, 72(2), 351–361.
Carstensen, L. L. (2006). The influence of a sense of time on human development. *Science*, 312, 1913–1915.
Carter, C. (2016). Still sucked into the body image thing: The impact of anti-ageing and health discourses on women's gendered identities. *Journal of Gender Studies*, 25(2), 200–214.
Caven, V., Lawley, S., & Baker, J. (2013). Performance, gender and sexualised work. *Equality, Diversity and Inclusion: An International Journal*, 32(5), 475–490.
Caza, B. B., Vough, H., & Puranik, H. (2018). Identity work in organisations and occupations: Definitions, theories and pathways forward. *Journal of Organizational Behaviour*, 39, 889–910.
Centre for Ageing Better. (2023). *Rumours of a 'Great Unretirement' are not just premature – they're damaging*. https://ageing-better.org.uk/blogs/rumours-great-unretirement-damaging.
Clarke, C., Brown, A., & Hailey, V. (2009). Working identities? Antagonistic discursive resources and managerial identity. *Human Relations*, 62(3), 323–352.
Corley, K. G., & Gioia, D. A. (2004). Identity ambiguity and change in the wake of a corporate spin-off. *Administrative Science Quarterly*, 49(2), 173–208.
Costas, J., & Fleming, P. (2009). Beyond dis-identification: A discursive approach to self-alienation in contemporary organization. *Human Relations*, 62(3), 353–378.
Coupland, C., & Brown, A. D. (2012). Identities in action: Processes and outcomes. *Scandinavian Journal of Management*, 28(1), 1–4.
Coupland, C., Brown, A. D., Daniels, K., & Humphreys, M. (2008). Saying it with feeling: Analysing speakable emotions. *Human Relations*, 61(3), 327–353.
Crawford, R. (2006). Health as a meaningful social practice. *Health*, 10(4), 401–420.
Criado-Perez, C. (2019). *Invisible women: Data bias in a world designed for men*, 1–272. New York, NY: Harry N. Abrams.
Cutcher, L., & Achtel, P. (2017). 'Doing the brand': Aesthetic labour as situated, relational performance in fashion retail. *Work, Employment and Society*, 31(4), 675–691.
Damaske, S. (2011). *For the family? How class and gender shape women's work*. New York, NY: Oxford University Press.
Damaske, S., & Frech, A. (2016). Women's work pathways across the life course. *Demography*, 53, 365–391.

Down, S., & Reveley, J. (2009). Between narration and interaction: Situating first-line supervisor identity work. *Human Relations*, 62(3), 379–401.

Duncan, C., & Loretto, W. (2004). Never the right age? Gender and age-based discrimination in employment. *Gender, Work & Organization*, 11(1), 95–115.

Duncan, C., White, P., & Loretto, W. (2000). Ageism and employment: Controversies, ambiguities and younger people's perceptions. *Ageing & Society*, 20, 279–302.

Durbin, S., & Tomlinson, J. (2014). Careers, mentors and role models for female part-time managers. *Gender, Work & Organization*, 21, 308–320. https://doi.org/10.1111/gwao.12038

Edge, C., Cooper, A., & Coffey, M. (2017). Barriers and facilitators to extended working lives in Europe: A gender focus. *Public Health Reviews*, 38(2), 1–27.

Emirbayer, M., & Johnson, V. (2008). Bourdieu and organizational analysis. *Theory & Society*, 37, 1–44.

Emslie, C., & Hunt, K. (2009). Live to work or work to live? A qualitative study of gender and work-life balance among women in mid-life. *Gender, Work & Organization*, 16(1), 151–172.

English Longitudinal Study of Ageing (ELSA). (2024). https://www.elsa-project.ac.uk/.

Entwistle, J. (2000). *The fashioned body: Fashion, dress and modern social theory*. Cambridge: Polity Press.

Fawcett Society. (2023). *Equal pay day 2023: Making flexible working the default.* https://www.fawcettsociety.org.uk/equal-pay-day-2023#:~:text=Making%20Flexible%20Work%20the%20Default,%C2%A36888%20p%2Fa).

The Ferret. (2023). *Women wait longer than men for emergency medical care in Scotland despite the fact they are more likely to be admitted to hospital after being seen in A&E*. Published in the ferret: https://theferret.scot/longer-ae-waits-disadvantage-women-figures-show/

Fineman, S. (2000). *Emotion in organizations*. Thousand Oaks, CA: Sage.

Fineman, S. (2003). *Understanding emotion at work*. London: Sage.

Fischer, A. H. (1993). Emotions and gender: A conceptual model of emotions in social interaction. In *Recent trends in theoretical psychology: Selected proceedings of the fourth biennial conference of the international society for theoretical psychology*, 325–332. New York, NY: Springer New York.

Ford, J., & Harding, N. (2011). The impossibility of the 'true self' of authentic leadership. *Leadership*, 7(4), 463–479.

Foweraker, B., & Cutcher, L. (2019). An ageless gift: Reciprocity and value creation by and for workers in mid to later life. *Work, Employment and Society*, 095001701984152, 1–17.

Freund, A. M. (2006). Age-differential motivational consequences of optimization versus compensation focus in younger and older adults. *Psychology and Aging*, 21(2), 240–252.

Freund, A. M. (2008). Successful aging as management of resources: The role of selection, optimization, and compensation. *Research in Human Development*, 5(2), 94–106.

Freund, A. M., & Baltes, P. B. (2002). The adaptiveness of selection, optimization, and compensation as strategies of life management: Evidence from a preference study on proverbs. *Journal of Gerontology*, 57B(5), 426–434.

Frevert, T. K., & Walker, L. S. (2014). Physical attractiveness and social status. *Sociology Compass*, 8, 313–323.

García-Jiménez, M., Torres-Enamorado, D., Sánchez-Sánchez, E., García-Gil, C., & Casado-Mejía, R. (2024). Caring for others without neglecting oneself? Grandparent caregivers, gender, and perceived health-related quality of life. *Health Care for Women International*, 1–20.

Gibson, D. E., & Barron, L. A. (2003). Exploring the impact of role models on older employees. *Career Development International*, 8(4), 198–209.

Gioia, D. A., Corley, K. G., & Hamilton, A. L. (2012). Seeking qualitative rigor in inductive research: Notes on the Gioia Methodology. *Organization Research Methods*, 16(1), 15–31.

Gjellestad, M., Haraldstad, K., Enehaug, H., & Helmersen, M. (2023). Women's health and working life: A scoping review. *International Journal of Environmental Research and Public Health*, 20(2), 1080.

Goldman, B. M., & Kernis, M. H. (2002). The role of authenticity in healthy psychological functioning and subjective well-being. *Annals of the American Psychotherapy Association*, 5(6), 18–20.

Gordon, R. A., & Arvey, R. D. (2004). Age bias in laboratory and field settings: A meta-analytic investigation. (Author Abstract). *Journal of Applied Social Psychology*, 34, 468.

Gordon, S. L. (1989). Institutional and impulsive orientations in selectively appropriating emotions to self. In *The sociology of emotions: Original essays and research papers*, 115–135. Greenwich, CT: Jai Press.

Goretzki, L., & Messner, M. (2019). Backstage and frontstage interactions in management accountants' identity work. *Accounting, Organizations and Society*, 74, 1–20.

Grandey, A. A., Gabriel, A. S., & King, E. B. (2020). Tackling taboo topics: A review of the three M's in working women's lives. *Journal of Management*, 46(1), 7–35.

Gray, B., & Kish-Gephart, J. J. (2013). Encountering social class differences at work: How 'class work' perpetuates inequality. *Academy of Management Review*, 38(4), 670–699.

Griffiths, A., MacLennan, S. J., & Hassard, J. (2013). Menopause and work: An electronic survey of employees' attitudes in the UK. *Mauritas*, 76, 155–159.

The Guardian. (February 2023). *Women work two months for free*. www.theguardian.com/business/2023/feb/23/women-work-two-months-for-free-reveals-tuc-analysis. Accessed on 28/2/23.

Hamermesh, D. S. (2011). *Beauty pays: Why attractive people are more successful*. Princeton, NJ: Princeton University Press.

Hamermesh, D. S., & Biddle, J. (1994). Beauty and the labor market. *American Economic Review*, 84, 1174–1194.

Hardy, C., Griffiths, A., Norton, S., & Hunter, M. S. (2018). Self-help cognitive behavior therapy for working women with problematic hot flushes and night sweats: A multicenter randomized controlled trial. *Menopause*, 25, 508.

Heilman, M. E. (1983). Sex bias in work settings: The lack of fit model. *Research in Organizational Behavior*, 5, 269–298.

Heilman, M. E. (1997). Sex discrimination and the affirmative action remedy: The role of sex stereotypes. *Journal of Business Ethics*, 16, 877–889.

Heilman, M. E., Martell, R. F., & Simon, M. C. (1988). The vagaries of sex bias: Conditions regulating the undervaluation, equivaluation, and overvaluation of female job applicants. *Organizational Behavior and Human Decision Processes*, 41, 98–110.

Hickey, M., Riach, K., Kachouie, R., & Jack, G. (2017). No sweat: Managing menopausal symptoms at work. *Journal of Psychosomatic Obstetrics and Gynecology*, 38, 202–209.

Hill, A. (2023). *'Blind spots' revealed as UK's top firms have women in just one in five commercial roles*. www.theguardian.com/business/2023/nov/27/gender-parity-study-pipeline-uk-companies-women-commercial-roles. Accessed on 9/2/24

Hosoda, M., Stone-Romero, E. F., & Coats, G. (2003). The effects of physical attractiveness on job-related outcomes: A meta-analysis of experimental studies. *Personnel Psychology*, 56, 431–462.

Howlett, N., Pine, K., Cahill, N., Orakçioğlu, İ., & Fletcher, B. (2015). Unbuttoned: The interaction between provocativeness of female work attire and occupational status. *A Journal of Research*, 72, 105–116.
Huff, A. S. (2009). *Designing research for publication*. Thousand Oaks, CA: Sage.
Hurd, L. C. (1999). 'We're not old!': Women in mid to later life's negotiation of aging and oldness. *Journal of Aging Studies*, 13(4), 419–439.
Hurd Clarke, L. H. (2010). *Facing age: Women growing older in anti-aging culture*. Lanham, MD: Rowman & Littlefield.
Hurd Clarke, L. H. (2018). Women, aging, and beauty culture: Navigating the social perils of looking old. *Generations*, 41(4), 104–110.
Hurd Clarke, L. H., & Griffin, M. (2008). Visible and invisible ageing: Beauty work as a response to ageism. *Ageing & Society*, 28(5), 653–674.
Hurd Clarke, L. H., & Korotchenko, A. (2016). 'I know it exists . . . but I haven't experienced it personally': Older Canadian men's perceptions of ageism as a distant social problem. *Ageing & Society*, 36(8), 1757–1773.
Ibarra, H. (1999). Provisional selves: Experimenting with image and identity in professional adaptation. *Administrative Science Quarterly*, 44(4), 764–791.
Ibarra, H. (2015). The authenticity paradox. *Harvard Business Review*, 93(1/2), 53–59.
Ibarra, H., & Barbulescu, R. (2010). Identity as narrative: Prevalence, effectiveness, and consequences of narrative identity work in macro work role transitions. *Academy of Management Review*, 35, 135–154.
Ibarra, H., & Obodaru, O. (2016). Betwixt and between identities: Liminal experience in contemporary careers. *Research in Organizational Behaviour*, 36, 47–64.
Ibarra, H., & Petriglieri, J. (2007). *Impossible selves: Image strategies and identity threat in professional women's career transitions*. INSEAD Working Paper, 2007/69/OB.
International Longevity Centre. (2019). https://ilcuk.org.uk/maximising-the-longevity-dividend/.pdf
Isopahkala-Bouret, U. (2017). 'It's a great benefit to have gray hair!': The intersection of gender, aging, and visibility in midlife professional women's narratives. *Journal of Women & Aging*, 29, 267–277.
Jack, G., Bariola, E., Riach, K., Schnapper, J., & Pitts, M. (2014). Work, women and the menopause: An Australian exploratory study. *Climacteric*, 17(Suppl 2), 34.
Jack, G., Riach, K., Bariola, E., Pitts, M., Schapper, J., & Sarrel, P. (2016). Menopause in the workplace: What employers should be doing. *Maturitas*, 85, 88–95.
Johnson, P., & Duberley, J. (2003). Reflexivity in management research. *Journal of Management Studies*, 40(5), 1279–1303.
Johnson, S. K., Podratz, K. E., Dipboye, R. L., & Gibbons, E. (2010). Physical attractiveness biases in ratings of employment suitability: Tracking down the 'beauty is beastly' effect. *The Journal of Social Psychology*, 150, 301–318.
Jones, K. P., Arena, D. F., Nittrouer, C. L., Alonso, N. M., & Lindsey, A. P. (2017). Subtle discrimination in the workplace: A vicious cycle. *Industrial and Organisational Psychology*, 10(1), 51–76.
Jones, K. P., & Clifton, J. (2018). Rendering sexism invisible in workplace narratives: A narrative analysis of female entrepreneurs' stories of not being talked to by men. *Gender, Work & Organization*, 25, 557–574.
Jones, K. P., Peddie, C. I., Gilrane, V. L., King, E. B., & Gray, A. (2016). Not so subtle: A meta-analysis of the correlates of subtle and overt discrimination. *Journal of Management*, 42, 1588–1613.
Jones, L., Cook, R., & Connolly, S. (2023). Parenthood and job quality: Is there a motherhood penalty in the UK? *Social Indicators Research*, 170(2), 765–792.

Jyrkinen, M., & McKie, L. (2012). Gender, age and ageism: Experiences of women managers in finland and scotland. *Work, Employment and Society*, 26(1), 61–77.

Kalwij, A., & Vermeulen, F. (2008). Health and labour force participation of older people in Europe: What do objective health indicators add to the analysis? *Health Economics*, 17, 619–638.

Kerr, R., & Robinson, S. (2011). Leadership as an elite field: Scottish banking leaders and the crisis of 2007–2009. *Leadership*, 7(2), 151–173.

Koch, A. J., D'Mello, S. D., & Sackett, P. R. (2015). A meta-analysis of gender stereotypes and bias in experimental simulations of employment decision making. *Journal of Applied Psychology*, 100, 128–161.

Kooij, D. T. A. M., De Lange, A. H., Jansen, P. G. W., Kanfer. R., & Dikkers, J. S. E. (2011). Age and work-related motives: Results of a meta-analysis. *Journal of Organizational Behavior*, 32, 197–225.

Kornberger, M., & Brown, A. (2007). 'Ethics' as a discursive resource for identity work. *Human Relations*, 60(3), 497–518.

Kotter-Grühn, D., Kornadt, A. E., & Stephan, Y. (2016). Looking beyond chronological age: Current knowledge and future directions in the study of subjective age. *Gerontology*, 62(1), 86–93.

Krekula, C. (2007). The intersection of age and gender: Reworking gender theory and social gerontology. *Current Sociology*, 55, 155–171.

Krekula, C. (2009). Age coding: On age-based practices of distinction. *International Journal of Ageing and Later Life*, 4(2), 7–31.

Krekula, C. (2016). Contextualizing women in mid to later life's body images: Time dimensions, multiple reference groups, and age codings of appearance. *Journal of Women & Aging*, 28(1), 58–67.

Krumhuber, E., Manstead, A. S. R., Cosker, D., Marshall, D., Rosin, P. L., & Kappas, A. (2007). Facial dynamics as indicators of trustworthiness and cooperative behavior. *Emotion*, 7, 730–735.

Kuhn, T. (2009). Positioning lawyers: Discursive resources, professional ethics and identification. *Organization*, 16(5), 681–704.

Langlois, J. H., Kalakanis, L., Rubenstein, A. J., Larson, A., Hallam, M., & Smoot, M. (2000). Maxims or myths of beauty? A meta-analytic and theoretical review. *Psychological Bulletin*, 126, 390–423.

Livingstone, D. W., & Scholtz, A. (2016). Reconnecting class and production relations in an advanced capitalist 'knowledge economy': Changing class structure and class consciousness. *Capital & Class*, 40(3), 169–493.

Loretto, W., & Vickerstaff, S. (2013). The domestic and gendered context for retirement. *Human Relations*, 66(1), 65–86.

Loretto, W., & Vickerstaff, S. (2015). Gender, age and flexible working in later life. *Work, Employment and Society*, 29(2), 233–249.

Loretto, W., & White, P. (2006). Work, more work and retirement: Workers in mid to later life' perspectives. *Social Policy & Society*, 5(4), 495–506.

Maestripieri, D., Henry, A., & Nickels, N. (2017). Explaining financial and prosocial biases in favor of attractive people: Interdisciplinary perspectives from economics, social psychology, and evolutionary psychology. *Behavioural and Brain Sciences*, 40, 1–56.

Maestripieri, D., Klimczuk, A. C. E., Traficonte, D. M., & Wilson, M. C. (2014). A greater decline in female facial attractiveness during middle age reflects women's loss of reproductive value. *Frontiers in Psychology*, 5, 1–6.

Magee, C. A., Heaven, P. C. L., & Miller, L. M. (2013). Personality change predicts self-reported mental and physical change. *Journal of Personality*, 81(3), 324–334.

Marcinkus Murphy, W. (2012). Reverse mentoring at work: Fostering cross-generational learning and developing millennial leaders. *Human Resource Management*, 51(4), 549–573.

Marsh, K., & Musson, G. (2008). Men at work and at home: Managing emotion in telework. *Gender, Work & Organization*, 15, 31–48.

Martinson, M., & Berridge, C. (2015). Successful ageing and its discontents: A systematic review of the social gerontology literature. *The Gerontologist*, 55(1), 58–69.

Mavin, S. A., Elliott, C., Stead, V., & William, J. (2016). Women managers, leaders and the media gaze: Learning from popular culture, autobiographies, broadcast and media press. *Gender in Management: An International Journal*, 31(5/6), 314–321.

McMullin, J. A., & Cairney, J. (2004). Self-esteem and the intersection of age, class, and gender. *Journal of Aging Studies*, 18, 75–90.

Meister, A., Jehn, K. A., & Thatcher, S. M. (2014). Feeling misidentified: The consequences of internal identity asymmetries for individuals at work. *Academy of Management Review*, 39(4), 488–512.

Meister, A., Sinclair, A., & Jehn, K. A. (2017). Identities under scrutiny: How women leaders navigate feeling misidentified at work. *The Leadership Quarterly*, 28(5), 672–690.

Meyer, J. H., & Land, R. (2006). Threshold concepts and troublesome knowledge: Issues of liminality. In *Overcoming barriers to student understanding*, 43–56. Abingdon, UK: Routledge.

Miscenko, D., & Day, D. V. (2016). Identity and identification at work. *Organizational Psychology Review*, 6(3), 215–247.

Mobius, M. M., & Rosenblat, T. S. (2006). Why beauty matters. *American Economic Review*, 96, 222–235.

Moya-Garofano, A., & Moya, M. (2019). Focusing on one's own appearance leads to body shame in women but not for men: The mediating role of body surveillance and appearance-contingent self-worth. *Body Image*, 29, 58–64.

Ng, T. W. H., & Feldman, D. C. (2012). Evaluating six common stereotypes about workers in mid to later life with meta-analytical data. *Personnel Psychology*, 65, 821–858.

Nickson, D. (2018). The importance of how you look for getting in and getting on in the workplace. In Broadbridge, & Fieldon (Eds.), *Research handbook of diversity and careers*. Cheltenham: Edward Elgar.

Nickson, D., Timming, A. R., Re, D., & Perrett, D. I. (2016). Subtle Increases in BMI within a healthy weight range still reduce womens' employment chances in the service sector. *PLoS One*, 11, e0159659.

Nico, M. L. (2016). Bringing life back into life research: Using the life grid as a research instrument for qualitative data collection and analysis. *Quality and Quantity*, 50, 2107–2120.

Office for National Statistics. (2016). *Labour force survey, Q3 2015–2016*. London: ONS. www.ons.gov.uk/employmentandlabourmarket/peopleinwork/employmentandemployeetypes/bulletins/uklabourmarket/february2016

Office for National Statistics. (2023). *Gender pay gap in the UK: 2023*. www.ons.gov.uk/employmentandlabourmarket/peopleinwork/earningsandworkinghours/bulletins/genderpaygapintheuk/2023

Organisation for Economic Co-operation and Development (OECD). (October 2023). *The midcareer opportunity*. www.oecd.org/employment/ageingandemployment-policies.htm#:~:text=Making%20successful%20career%20transitions%2C%20however,jobs%20that%20employers%20may%20provide

Parry, O., Thomson, C., & Fowkes, G. (1999). Life course data collection: Qualitative interviewing using the life grid. *Sociological Research Online*, 4(2), 102–112.

Peluchette, J. V., & Karl, K. (2007). The impact of workplace attire on employee self-perceptions. *Human Resource Development Quarterly*, 18(3), 345–360.

Petriglieri, J. L. (2011). Under threat: Responses to and the consequences of threats to individuals' identities. *Academy of Management Review*, 36(4), 641–662.

Phelan, A. (2018). Researching ageism through discourse. In *Contemporary perspectives on ageism*, 549–564. Cham: Springer.

Powroznik, K. M. (2017). Healthism and weight-based discrimination: The unintended consequences of health promotion in the workplace. *Work and Occupations*, 44(2), 139–170.

Price, D., Glaser, K., Ginn, J., & Nicholls, M. (2016). How important are state transfers for reducing poverty rates in later life? *Ageing & Society*, 36(9), 1794–1825.

Quental, C., Rojas Gaviria, P., & del Bucchia, C. (2023). The dialectic of (menopause) zest: Breaking the mold of organizational irrelevance. *Gender, Work & Organization*, 30, 1816–1838.

Riach, K. (2007). 'Othering' older worker identity in recruitment. *Human Relations*, 60(11), 1701–1726.

Riach, K., & Cutcher, L. (2014). Built to last: Ageing, class and the masculine body in a UK hedge fund. *Work, Employment and Society*, 28(5), 771–787.

Riach, K., & Loretto, W. (2009). Identity work and the 'unemployed' worker: Age, disability and the lived experience of the older unemployed. *Work, Employment and Society*, 23, 102–119.

Riach, K., Loretto, W., & Krekula, C. (2015). Gendered ageing in the new economy: Introduction to special issue of gender, work and organization. *Gender, Work & Organization*, 22(5), 437–444.

Riach, K., Rumens, N., & Tyler, M. (2016). Towards a Butlerian methodology: Undoing organisational performativity through anti-narrative research. *Human Relations*, 69(11), 2069–2089.

Roscigno, V. J., Mong, S., Byron, R., & Tester, G. (2007). Age discrimination, social closure and employment. *Social Forces*, 86(1), 313–329.

Rowe, J. W., & Kahn, R. L. (1997). *Successful aging*. New York: Pantheon Books.

Rowe, J. W., & Kahn, R. L. (2015). Successful ageing 2.0: Conceptual expansions for the 21st Century. *The Journals of Gerontology*, 70(4), 593–596.

Rudolph, C. W. (2016). Lifespan development perspective on working: A literature review of motivational theories. *Work, Aging and Retirement*, 2(2), 130–158.

Ryan, C., Bergin, M., & Wells, J. S. (2017). Valuable yet vulnerable – A review of the challenges encountered by older nurses in the workplace. *International Journal of Nursing Studies*, 72, 42–52.

Sabelis, I., & Schilling, E. (2013). Editorial: Frayed careers: Exploring rhythms of working lives. *Gender, Work & Organization*, 20(2), 127–133.

Sanders, M. J., & McCready, J. W. (2010). Does work contribute to successful aging outcomes in workers in mid to later life? *The International Journal of Aging and Human Development*, 71, 209–229.

Saunders, M. N. K., & Townsend, K. (2016). Reporting and justifying the number of interview participants in organisation and workplace research. *British Journal of Management*, 27, 836–852.

Savage, M. (2015). *Social class in the 21st century*. London: Pelican Books.

Sayer, A. (2005). Class, moral worth and recognition. *Sociology*, 39(5), 947–963.

Schein, V. E. (1975). Relationships between sex role stereotypes and requisite management characteristics among female managers. *Journal of Applied Psychology*, 60(3), 340–344.

Schein, V. E. (2001). A global look at psychological barriers to women's progress in management. *Journal of Social Issues*, 57(4), 675–688.

Schein, V. E. (2007). Women in management: Reflections and projections. *Women in Management Review*, 22(1), 6–18.
Schein, V. E., & Mueller, R. (1992). Sex role stereotyping and requisite management characteristics: A cross-cultural look. *Journal of Organizational Behavior*, 13(5), 439 447.
Schilling, E. (2015). 'Success is satisfaction with what you have'? Biographical work – Life balance of older female employees in public administration. *Gender, Work & Organization*, 22(5), 474–489.
Schofield, D., Cunich, M., Kelly, S., Passey, M. E., Shrestha, R., Callander, E., Tanton, R., & Veerman, L. (2015). The impact of diabetes on the labour force participation, savings and retirement income of workers aged 45–64 years in Australia. *PLoS One*, 10(2), e0116860.
Sealy, R. H., & Singh, V. (2010). The importance of role models and demographic context for senior women's work identity development. *International Journal of Management Reviews*, 12(3), 284–300.
Shaw, R., & Langman, M. (2017). Perceptions of being old and the ageing process. *Ageing International*, 42, 115–135.
Skeggs, B. (1997). *Formations of class and gender: Becoming respectable*. London: Sage.
Skeggs, B. (2004). Pierre Bourdieu's analysis of class, gender and sexuality. *Sociological Review*, 1–31.
Slevin, K. F. (2010). If I had lots of money . . . I'd have a body makeover: Managing the aging body. *Social Forces*, 88(3), 1003–1020. https://doi.org/10.1353/sof.0.0302
Sloane, J. (2023). *Aging on screen and on the page: Changing depictions of older people in the media*. www.asc.upenn.edu/news-events/news/aging-screen-and-page-changing-depictions-older-people-media#:~:text=The%20way%20aging%20is%20portrayed,societal%20value%20and%20erotic%20appeal. Accessed on 30/1/24.
Snow, D. A., & Anderson, L. (1987). Identity work among the homeless: The verbal construction and avowal of personal identities. *American Journal of Sociology*, 92(6), 1336–1371.
Sontag. S. (1979). The double standard of ageing. In J. Williams (Ed.), *Psychology of women*, 462–478. New York: Academic Press.
Statista. (2023). www.statista.com/statistics/802183/annual-pay-employees-in-the-uk/. Accessed on 15/2/24.
Steffan, B. (2021). Managing menopause at work: The contradictory nature of identity talk. *Gender, Work & Organization*, 28(1), 195–214.
Steffan, B., & Potočnik, K. (2023). Teaching through the menopause: A flexible work paradox. In *Teachers and teaching post-COVID*, 64–86. Abingdon, UK: Routledge.
Strawbridge, W. J., Wallhagen, M. I., & Cohen, R. D. (2002). Successful aging and well-being: Self-rated compared with Rowe and Kahn. *Gerontologist*, 42, 727–733.
Stryker, S. (2004). Integrating emotion into identity theory. In J. H. Turner (Ed.), *Theory and research on human emotions* (Advances in Group Processes), Vol. 21, 1–23. Bingley: Emerald Group Publishing Limited.
Sveningsson, S., & Alvesson, M. (2003). Managing managerial identities: Organizational fragmentation, discourse and identity struggle. *Human Relations*, 56(10), 1163–1193.
Swail, J., & Marlow, S. (2018). Embrace the masculine; attenuate the feminine – Gender, identity work and entrepreneurial legitimation in the nascent context. *Entrepreneurship & Regional Development*, 30(1–2), 256–282.

Taylor, P., Loretto, W., Marshall, V., Earl, C., & Phillipson, C. (2016). The older worker: Identifying a critical research agenda. *Social Policy & Society*, 15(4), 675–689.

Terry, J. (2020). 'In the middle': A qualitative study of talk about mental health nursing roles and work. *International Journal of Mental Health Nursing*, 29, 414–426. https://doi.org/10.1111/inm.12676

Thomas, R., Hardy, C., Cutcher, L., & Ainsworth, S. (2014). What's age got to do with it? On the critical analysis of age and organisations. *Organization Studies*, 35(11), 1569–1584.

Thomas, R., & Linstead, A. (2002). Losing the plot? Middle managers and identity. *Organization*, 9(1), 71–93.

Trethewey, A. (1999). Disciplined bodies: Women's embodied identities at work. *Organization Studies*, 20(3), 423–450.

Trethewey, A. (2000). Reproducing and resisting the master narrative of decline. *Management Communication Quarterly*, 15(2), 183–226.

Truxillo, D. M., Cadiz, D. M., & Hammer, L. B. (2015). Supporting the ageing workforce: A review and recommendations for workplace intervention research. *Annual Review of Organisational Psychology and Organisational Behaviour*, 2, 351–381.

Tulle, E. (2008). The ageing body and the ontology of ageing: Athletic competence in later life. *Body and Society*, 14(3), 1–19.

Tulle, E., & Krekula, C. (2013). Ageing embodiment and the search for social change. *International Journal of Ageing and Later Life*, 8(1), 7–10.

Turner, V. (1969). *The ritual process: Structure and anti-structure*. London: Routledge & Kegan Paul.

Twigg, J. (2004). The body, gender, and age: Feminist insights in social gerontology. *Journal of Ageing Studies*, 18, 59–73.

Twigg, J. (2007). Clothing, age and the body: A critical review. *Ageing & Society*, 27, 385–305.

Twigg, J. (2012). Adjusting the cut: Fashion, the body and age on the UK high street. *Ageing & Society*, 32, 1030–1054.

UK Biobank. (2024). https://www.ukbiobank.ac.uk/enable-your-research/about-our-data/questionnaire-data

UK Government. (February 2023). *DWP leads way supporting people aged over 50 at work*. www.gov.uk/government/news/dwp-leads-way-supporting-people-aged-over-50-at-work

UK Parliament. (March 2023). *Why have older workers left the labour market?* https://commonslibrary.parliament.uk/why-have-older-workers-left-the-labour-market/. Accessed on 12/12/23.

UK Parliament. (March 2024). *Rising cost of living crisis in the UK*. https://commonslibrary.parliament.uk/research-briefings/cbp-9428/. Accessed on 1/4/24.

Understanding Society. (2023). https://www.understandingsociety.ac.uk/news/2023/11/22/understanding-society-wave-13/

Unson, C., & Richardson, M. (2012). Insights into the experiences of workers in mid to later life and change: Through the lens of selection, optimisation and compensation. *The Gerontologist*, 53(3), 484–494.

Vaes, J., Paladino, P., & Puvia, E. (2011). Are sexualized women complete human beings? Why women dehumanize sexually objectified women. *European Journal of Social Psychology*, 41, 774–785.

Wacquant, L. (2008). *Urban outcasts: A comparative sociology of advanced marginality*. Polity.

Warhurst, C., & Nickson, D. (2007). Employee experience of aesthetic labour in retail and hospitality. *Work, Employment and Society*, 21(1), 103–120.

Warhurst, C., & Nickson, D. (2009). 'Who's got the look?' Emotional, aesthetic and sexualized labour in interactive services. *Gender, Work & Organization*, 16(3), 385–404.

Warhurst, C., van den Broek, D., Hall, R., & Nickson, D. (2009). Lookism: The new frontier of employment discrimination? *Journal of Industrial Relations*, 51(1), 131–136.

Webster, M., & Driskell, J. E. (1983). Beauty as status. *American Journal of Sociology*, 89, 140–165.

Winkelmann-Gleed, A. (2012). Retirement or committed to work? Conceptualising prolonged labour market participation through organisational commitment. *Employee Relations*, 34(1), 80–90.

Winkler, I. (2018). Identity work and emotions: A review. *International Journal of Management Reviews*, 20, 120–133.

Ybema, S., Keenoy, T., Oswick, C., Beverungen, A., Ellis, N., & Sabelis, I. (2009). Articulating identities. *Human Relations*, 62, 299–322.

Zacher, H. (2013). Older job seekers' job search intensity: The interplay of proactive personality, age and occupational future time perspective. *Ageing & Society*, 33, 1139–1166.

Zacher, H. (2015). Successful aging at work. *Work, Aging and Retirement*, 1(1), 4–25.

Index

Note: Numbers in **bold** indicate a table. Numbers in *italics* indicate a figure on the corresponding page.

For Product Safety Concerns and Information please contact our EU representative GPSR@taylorandfrancis.com Taylor & Francis Verlag GmbH, Kaufingerstraße 24, 80331 München, Germany